# INTERACTIVE LISTENING ON CAMPUS

# INTERACTIVE LISTENING ON CAMPUS

## Authentic Academic Mini-Lectures

**GARY JAMES**
**Honolulu Community College**

**HEINLE & HEINLE PUBLISHERS**
**A Division of Wadsworth, Inc.**
**Boston, Massachusetts 02116 U.S.A.**

Vice President and Publisher: Stanley J. Galek
Editorial Director: David C. Lee
Assistant Editor: Kenneth Mattson
Project Manager: Stacey Sawyer, Sawyer & Williams
Production Supervisor: Patricia Jalbert
Manufacturing Coordinator: Lisa McLaughlin
Text Design: Nancy Benedict
Unit Opening Illustrations: Phil Frank
Interior Illustrations: Susan Detrich
Cover Design and Illustration: Christy L. Rosso

Manufactured in the United States of America.

Heinle & Heinle Publishers is a division of Wadsworth, Inc.

*Library of Congress Cataloging-in-Publication Data*

James, Gary, 1939–
    Interactive listening on campus : authentic academic mini-lectures
/ Gary James.
        p.    cm.
    Includes index.
    ISBN 0-8384-2270-5
    1. English in language—Textbooks for foreign speakers.   2. Lecture
method in teaching.   3. Listening.   I. Title.
PE1128.J29   1992
428.3′4—dc20                                                91-42683
                                                                CIP

ISBN 0-8384-2270-5

10   9   8   7   6   5   4

*Dedication*

In memory of my parents, Louis and Mildred James
and my friend, John Mark Summers

# CONTENTS

*Preface   ix*

# PREFACE

*Interactive Listening on Campus: Authentic Academic Mini-Lectures* provides intermediate-level ESL students opportunities to listen to mini-lectures about academic topics. The aim of these materials is to teach students how to listen and better understand the language used in the lecture hall.

This book is divided into two parts with ten units in each part. Each unit in Part One is composed of two mini-lectures (each ranging from two to three minutes in length) delivered by two different native speakers. The subject matter of the mini-lectures comes from a diverse sampling of academic disciplines including health, general science, business, engineering, psychology, computer science, and physics.

Each unit's lecturers address the same topic, resulting in a wide overlap of vocabulary. Students listen to each mini-lecture and complete various tasks to develop the following academic listening skills:

1. Listening for the main idea
   - identifying the main idea and its position in the passage
   - becoming aware of transitional phrases or signals that introduce the main idea
   - becoming aware of the different prosodic features (stress, pitch, volume) that differentiate the main idea from the rest of the passage

2. Notetaking
   - discriminating between important and unimportant words for note-taking purposes
   - becoming aware of various note-taking formats

Each unit in Part Two is composed of a single mini-lecture of two to three minutes in length. The topics of these mini-lectures are typically from the disciplines of zoology, general science, history, sociology, or speech and communication. The mini-lectures can be used for extra listening practice by students or for testing purposes by the instructor.

Each unit in Part One features the following components:

### Getting Set

- illustrations related to the topic of the mini-lectures with accompanying discussion questions

### Talking It Over

- an alphabetized list of topic-specific vocabulary items culled from the lesson's mini-lectures

### Spelling It Out

- definitions for five selected vocabulary items found in the mini-lectures and blanks for spelling them

### Checking It Off

- an identification exercise using the list from the "Talking It Over" section

### Zeroing In: Main Idea

- main idea and non-main-idea sentences listed in the order of their occurrence in the mini-lectures
- an alphabetized list of phrases used to introduce the main ideas
- questions about the prosodic features for each of the phrases used to introduce the main ideas
- a question regarding the relative position of the main ideas in the mini-lectures

### Practicing New Words

- selected vocabulary items from the mini-lectures with their definitions in a matching format
- selected vocabulary from the mini-lectures and sentences for filling in the correct word form
- selected vocabulary from the mini-lectures listed in a series with two similar items and a distractor
- selected vocabulary from the mini-lectures with questions about usage, derivation, prefixes, suffixes, and so on.

### Writing It Down

- summary sentences of the mini-lectures with blanks for writing down important words from that summary in various note-taking formats

### Following Up

- suggestions for an out-of-class homework assignment using the encyclopedia
- discussion suggestions to talk or write about
- examination of lecture transcript for main idea and vocabulary

Each unit in Part Two features these components:

### Getting Set

- same as Part One

### Talking It Over

- same as Part One

### Checking It Off

- same as Part One

### Zeroing In: Main Idea

- same as Part One

### Zeroing In: Supporting Details

- an alphabetized list of supporting detail sentences and non-supporting detail sentences from the mini-lecture

### In Other Words

- selected vocabulary items in sentences from the mini-lecture with their definitions in a multiple-choice format

### Writing It Down

- two summaries of the mini-lecture with blanks for writing down important words from the better one

### Following Up

- suggestions for an out-of-class homework assignment
- discussion suggestions to talk or write about
- examination of lecture transcript for main idea and vocabulary

# Acknowledgments

Until lessons are tried out with actual students in the give-and-take of the ESL classroom, materials writing—at least in the initial stages—can be a solitary experience. Such was not the case for this project.

At the outset I spent many hours with Bette Matthews as we brainstormed to lay the groundwork and structure for these materials. We even jointly wrote a sample lesson to see how the format would correlate with our ideas and objectives. This early collaboration was invaluable and kept me on track over the years as the materials evolved to their present form.

Since the lessons in this text are derived from extemporaneously delivered lectures, no materials could be written without first transcribing the lectures. My colleagues at Honolulu Community College were most generous in giving their time and expertise for many hours of audiorecording. I am grateful to Keith Crockett, Peg Eskola, Lei Lani Hinds, Ed Ketz, Bette Matthews, Wendy Pollitt, Ken Thern, and Chuck Whitley. Others who recorded earlier versions of lessons were Paul Ban, George Dixon, Muriel Fujii, Terry Haney, Joyce Henna, Gloria Hooper, Doric Little, Maureen O'Brien, and Sandi Wong. All these people provided a real service to my immigrant students, who became quite familiar with their voices.

Special thanks also go to Elton Ogoso, whose technical skills made the recordings possible, and to Kathy Langaman for her patience and perseverance in word processing. I'm also indebted to the following reviewers, whose comments were critical in the development of this book. They are Donald Campbell, University of the Pacific; Gilbert Couts, American University; Debra Deane, University of Akron; Daniele Dibie, California State University-Northridge; Kristie Kirkpatrick, Amarillo College; and Laura Latulippe, Western Michigan University. David Lee, Editorial Director at Heinle and Heinle, offered encouragement and suggestions that were much appreciated. On a personal note, I am very indebted to Paul Ban for his never-ending support and understanding.

# To The Student

The title of this text is *Interactive Listening on Campus: Authentic Academic Mini-Lectures.* Take a look at these words to better understand what the title means.

INTERACTIVE   An interactive group of people is one in which the people communicate about or work together on something. Much of the work you will do in this text will be done in pairs or small groups. You will begin to understand how much easier it is to learn something if you help someone else learn it too.

LISTENING ON CAMPUS   One of the most important skills needed in school is the ability to understand what the teacher is saying. You do not have to understand everything—only important points. This text will help you begin to understand how to find the main ideas while listening.

AUTHENTIC   If something is authentic, it is real. All the language heard on the cassette tape was spoken *first* and then written down *second.* If you begin to understand real language now, it will be easier for you in the future when you are sitting in a regular classroom.

ACADEMIC   Academic work is done in schools, colleges, and universities. There are many topics and subjects to study along with thousands of new vocabulary words. This text will help you begin to understand some of them.

MINI-LECTURES   Most teachers teach students by talking on a particular subject or giving a lecture. This text is made up of very short lectures. In each of the first ten units you will listen to two different people talk about the same thing.

HAPPY LISTENING!

*Gary James*

# PART ONE

TODAY'S LECTURE

Heat Transfer

# SECTION A

## Before You Listen

### Getting Set

These people are using heat energy.
How are the pictures the same?
How are they different?

## Talking It Over

You will hear a mini-lecture about heat transfer. Look at the following list of words. Practice saying them. Which words do you think that you will hear? Why? Discuss your answers.

| | | |
|---|---|---|
| brown | displaced | ovens |
| conduction | electromagnet waves | radiation |
| convection | energy | rise up |
| cooking | fire | source |
| cool | flame | sun |
| current | move (-d)(-ing) | warm(er) |

## Spelling It Out

Read the following definitions of some words from the mini-lecture. Listen to the words that match the definitions. Write down the spelling for each word.

1. __ __ __ __ __ __ : happens/takes place

2. __ __    __ __ __ __ __ __

   __ __ __ __ __ __ __

   __ __ __ __ : touching

3. __ __ __ __ __ __ __

   __ __ __ __ : hitting

4. __ __ __ __ __ __ : packed closely together

5. __ __    __

   __ __ __ __ __ __ __ __ __ __ : as a result

Now practice saying the words.

# As You Listen

 **Checking It Off**

Look at the vocabulary list above. Listen to the mini-lecture. <u>Underline</u> the words that you hear. Discuss your choices.

## Zeroing In: Main Idea

This mini-lecture has one main idea. Read the following sentences. Put an X in front of the most important point. Discuss your choice.

\_\_\_\_\_ 1. Heat is transferred between two bodies whenever the temperatures are not the same in those two bodies.

\_\_\_\_\_ 2. Conduction, convection, and radiation are the ways heat is transferred.

\_\_\_\_\_ 3. Heating a copper wire causes the atoms in the wire to move around more quickly.

\_\_\_\_\_ 4. When air is heated, it rises.

Look at the following phrases. They tell you that main ideas or important points will follow. Listen to the mini-lecture again. <u>Underline</u> the phrase that you hear. Discuss your answers.

1. In conclusion, then, I want you to understand that . . .
2. Today I'm going to be discussing . . .
3. What I want you to remember is . . .

Listen to this phrase from the mini-lecture. Answer the following questions. Discuss your answers.

1. What is the most important word? _____

2. Does the speaker say this word:

   quickly        slowly

3. Does the speaker say this word:

   loudly         softly

4. Listen to the mini-lecture again. Does the main idea come at the beginning, the middle, or the end?

# After You Listen

## Practicing New Words

■ The words on the left are from the mini-lecture. Practice saying them. Match the words with their definitions on the right. Discuss your answers.

|        |                        |    |                              |
|--------|------------------------|----|------------------------------|
| ——— 1. | unequal                | a. | allowed to go                |
| ——— 2. | distribution           | b. | be held up                   |
| ——— 3. | atoms                  | c. | giving out                   |
| ——— 4. | rapidly                | d. | in the end                   |
| ——— 5. | running around         | e. | is most likely               |
| ——— 6. | released               | f. | moving                       |
| ——— 7. | eventually             | g. | not the same                 |
| ——— 8. | molecules              | h. | quickly                      |
| ——— 9. | has a natural tendency | i. | small pieces of something    |
| ——— 10.| float                  | j. | smallest pieces of something |

■ Practice saying these words from the lecture. Some are adjectives and some are adverbs.

| Adjectives  | Adverbs    |
|-------------|------------|
| 1. direct   | directly   |
| 2. warm     | warmly     |
| 3. dense    | densely    |
| 4. natural  | naturally  |
| 5. eventual | eventually |
| 6. literal  | literally  |
| 7. rapid    | rapidly    |

■ Read the following sentences. Write the correct form of the word in the blank. Words from number one in the list above go in sentence number one below, words from number two on the list go in sentence number two, and so forth. <u>Circle</u> whether the word is an adjective or adverb.

1. a. Go ——————— down the walk to the Administration Building.

      adjective      adverb

   b. The campus map shows a more ——————— way to the library.

      adjective      adverb

2. a. The guest lecturer was greeted _____ by the
    students.  adjective    adverb

   b. _____ weather makes it difficult for me to study.
      adjective    adverb

3. a. The air is _____ with smoke from all those students
      smoking in the cafeteria.  adjective    adverb

   b. The classroom is _____ packed with students.
      adjective   adverb

4. a. Be as _____ as you can when you are making your
      presentation.  adjective    adverb

   b. Learning foreign languages comes _____ for her.
      adjective    adverb

5. a. _____ , good study habits will help you get good grades.
      adjective    adverb

   b. Failing the course is the _____ result of not coming to
      class.  adjective    adverb

6. a. Professor Matthews wants a _____ translation of the text.
      adjective    adverb

   b. She _____ helped him pass the course.
      adjective    adverb

7. a. A _____ review of notes just before the exam can be
      useful.  adjective    adverb

   b. We moved _____ through the course syllabus.
      adjective    adverb

■ Read and discuss the following questions with your classmates.

1. The lecturer used the word *current*, meaning "moving air." It also can
   mean "something belonging to the present time." Look at the
   following words from the lecture. Think of as many different
   meanings as you can.
   • transfer
   • bodies
   • run

2. The lecturer spoke about heat energy becoming **displaced** when a copper wire is heated. Can you think of any other things that can be displaced? What causes them to be displaced?

3. Air has the **natural tendency** to rise when heated. Complete the following chart.

| *Thing* | *Action* | *Natural tendency* |
|---------|----------|--------------------|
| air ⟶ | heated ⟶ | *rise* |
| air ⟶ | cooled ⟶ | |
| water ⟶ | boiled ⟶ | |
| water ⟶ | cooled to 0°C. (32°F.) ⟶ | |
| dog ⟶ | given food ⟶ | |
| plant ⟶ | kept in a dark room ⟶ | |

Can you think of some others?

## Writing It Down

Taking notes is a quick way to write down information. It is important because it helps us to remember the main ideas in a lecture. Read the following summary of the mini-lecture. Decide which words are the most important. (The sentence has six important words.) Cross out the words that are not important. Discuss your answers.

*The three ways by which heat can be moved from one place to another are conduction, convection, and radiation.*

There are many different ways to take notes. Here is one way. One blank means one word. Write the important words in the blanks.

_____  _____  _____ :

1. _____

2. _____

3. _____

 Listen to the mini-lecture one more time. Look at the notes while listening.

# SECTION B

## Before You Listen

### Spelling It Out

Read the following definitions of some words from the mini-lecture. Listen to the words that match the definition. Write down the spelling for each word.

1. _ _ _ _ _ _ _ _ : known

2. _ _ _ _ _ _ _ : thickness

3. _ _ _ _ _ _ _ _ _ _ : according to what is thought to be

4. _ _ _ _ _ _ _ : hit again and again

5. _ _ _ - _ _ - _ _ _

   _ _ _ _ _ _ _ _ : daily life

Now practice saying the words.

## As You Listen

 **Checking It Off**

Look at the vocabulary list on page 5. Listen to the mini-lecture. Circle the words that you hear. Discuss your answers with your classmates.

### Zeroing In: Main Idea

This mini-lecture has one main idea. Read the following sentences. Put an X in front of the most important point. Discuss your choice.

_____ 1. Heat can be moved from one place to another by conduction, convection, or radiation.

_____ 2. We have ovens that use conduction, convection, and radiation to transfer heat.

_____ 3. Conduction means that the heat is transferred directly from its source to the object.

_____ 4. A convection oven is a popular way of cooking these days.

 Look again at the phrases on page 6 that tell you that main ideas or important points will follow. Listen to the mini-lecture again. Circle the phrase that you hear. Discuss your answer.

Listen to this phrase from the mini-lecture. Answer the following questions. Discuss your answers.

1. What is the most important word? _____

2. Does the speaker say this word:

   quickly          slowly

3. Does the speaker say this word:

   loudly          softly

4. Listen to the mini-lecture again. Does the main idea come at the beginning, the middle, or the end?

# After You Listen

## Practicing New Words

■ The words on the left are from the mini-lecture. Practice saying them. Match the words with their definitions on the right. Discuss your answers.

| | |
|---|---|
| _____ 1. methods | a. all the same |
| _____ 2. decreases | b. becomes smaller |
| _____ 3. settles down | c. goes down |
| _____ 4. more evenly | d. influences |
| _____ 5. just | e. only |
| _____ 6. affects | f. ways |

■ Some of these words are from the mini-lecture. Look at each group, and circle the word or phrase that does not belong. What are the reasons for your answers?

| | | | |
|---|---|---|---|
| 1. discussing | speaking about | talking about | thinking about |
| 2. imagine | not forget | recall | remember |
| 3. habits | methods | procedures | ways |
| 4. familiar | known | not new | unknown |
| 5. directly | supposedly | without anything coming between | without stopping |
| 6. ending point | origin | source | starting point |
| 7. expensive | favored | popular | well liked |
| 8. a few | a number of | many | several |

■ Read and discuss the following questions with your classmates.

1. You can add *-ion* to many English words to make them nouns. Some examples are:

conduct ——————⟶ conduction
radiate ——————⟶ radiation
direct ——————⟶ direction

Can you think of some others?

2. The lecturer said that using a convection oven is a **popular** way of cooking these days. What other popular ways of doing things can you think of?

3. The lecturer said that radiant energy from the sun **affects** our **day-to-day existence**. What ways can you think of?

■ Taking notes is a quick way to write down information. It is important because it helps us to remember the main ideas in a lecture. Read the following summary of the mini-lecture. Decide which words are the most important. (The sentence has five important words.) Cross out the words that are not important. Discuss your answers.

*The transference of heat can be achieved in three different ways: by radiation, convection, or conduction. (5)*

■ There are many different ways to take notes. Here is one way. One blank means one word. Write the important words in the blanks.

_____     _____ —

—_____

—_____

—_____

 Listen to the mini-lecture one more time. Look at the notes while listening.

**Following Up**

1. Go to the library. Look up the section on "heat" in the encyclopedia. How does it explain the meanings for conduction, convection, and radiation? Copy a few words from the encyclopedia that explain each term.

   Conduction: _____

   _____

   _____

   Convection: _____

   _____

   _____

   Radiation: _____

   _____

   _____

2. Does the encyclopedia have any pictures or diagrams explaining how heat is transferred? If so, make photocopies and bring them to class.

3. List the source for your information:

   Name of encyclopedia _____

   Volume number _____ Year _____ Page(s) _____

4. Read the discussion suggestions, and choose one to talk or write about.
   a. Something which gives off heat is called a source of heat. There are six main sources of heat. What are they? What is the most important one?
   b. Heat is used in many ways in both home and industry. How many ways can you think of?

5. Read the transcripts of both mini-lectures. Highlight the main ideas. Highlight any vocabulary that you do not understand, and find the meanings. Listen to the mini-lectures and follow along with the transcripts.

TODAY'S LECTURE

Stress

# SECTION A

## Before You Listen

### Getting Set

What words can you think of that describe how the person in each picture feels?

Why does the person feel that way?

### Talking It Over

You will hear a mini-lecture about stress. Look at the following list of words. Practice saying them. Which words do you think that you will hear? Why? Discuss your answers.

| | | |
|---|---|---|
| bosses | fellow students | sibling |
| children | girlfriend | social |
| conflict | husband | strain |
| co-workers | noise pollution | teachers |
| crowding | parents | tension |
| disagreements | physical | wife |
| family | school | |

### Spelling It Out

Read the following definitions of some words from the mini-lecture. Listen to the words that match the definitions. Write down the spelling for each word.

1. — — — — — — — : gives the meaning for

2. — — — — — —

    — — — — : get away from

3. — — — — — — — — — — — — — : beliefs about what others should do, how others should act

4. — — — — — — —

    — — — : try to win

5. — — — — — — — — — — : correct or punish

Now practice saying the words.  .

# As You Listen

 **Checking It Off**

Look at the vocabulary list on page 16. Listen to the mini-lecture. <u>Underline</u> the words that you hear. Discuss your choices.

### Zeroing In: Main Idea

This mini-lecture has one main idea. Read the following sentences. Put an X in front of the most important point. Discuss your choice.

_____ 1. The dictionary gives the meaning of stress as mental or physical tension.

_____ 2. Stress coming from things around you and stress coming from people around you are the two kinds of situational stress.

_____ 3. Children in schools near airports have higher blood pressures than children in schools in more quiet areas.

_____ 4. Situational stresses can be more easily controlled than other stresses.

Look at the following phrases. They tell you that main ideas or important points will follow. Listen to the mini-lecture again. <u>Underline</u> the phrase that you hear. Discuss your answers.

1. And now to quickly review . . .

2. Let us today examine why . . .

3. The topic for today's lecture is . . .

 Listen to this phrase from the mini-lecture. Answer the following questions. Discuss your answers.

1. What is the most important word? _____

2. Does the speaker say this word:

   quickly          slowly

3. Does the speaker say this word:

   loudly          softly

4. Listen to the mini-lecture again. Does the main idea come at the beginning, the middle, or the end?

# After You Listen

## Practicing New Words

■ The words on the left are from the mini-lecture. Practice saying them. Match the words with their definitions on the right. Discuss your answers.

_____ 1. mental               a. able to do something well

_____ 2. value systems        b. beliefs about what is important

_____ 3. family members       c. dealings between

_____ 4. frustrated           d. having to do with the mind

_____ 5. affection            e. love

_____ 6. competent            f. mothers, fathers, daughters, sons

_____ 7. sensitive            g. quick to notice and understand

_____ 8. interactions         h. unhappy

■ Practice saying these words from the lecture. Some are nouns and some are verbs.

| Nouns | Verbs |
|---|---|
| 1. definition | define |
| 2. pollution | pollute |
| 3. disagreement | disagree |
| 4. expectation | expect |
| 5. disappointment | disappoint |
| 6. competition | compete |
| 7. interaction | interact |

■ Read the following sentences. Write the correct form of the word in the blank. Words from number one in the list above go in sentence number one below, words from number two on the list go in sentence number two, and so forth. Circle whether the word is a noun or verb.

1. a. Let me _____ the word for you.   noun   verb

   b. Please give me your _____ of the term.   noun   verb

2. a. One can _____ the physical environment with all kinds of things.   noun   verb

   b. We can find noise _____ almost everywhere.   noun   verb

3. a. Class members had a _____ about how to do the assignment.   noun   verb

   b. Family members sometimes _____ about how to do things.   noun   verb

4. a. Teachers _____ students to do homework every night.   noun   verb

   b. The professor's _____ for the class was very high.   noun   verb

5. a. Don't be a _____ to your parents.   noun   verb

   b. If you _____ the instructor, she will let you know.   noun   verb

6. a. A _____ for the best essay was announced.   noun   verb

    b. Each group will _____ for the best grade.   noun   verb

7. a. Group members did not _____ with each other very well.
noun   verb

    b. Unfortunately, my _____ with fellow students was
stressful.   noun   verb

■ Read and discuss the following questions with your classmates.

1. The lecturer said that studies have found **direct connections** between the level of noise around people and their health problems. Can you think of other health problems directly connected to something else?

2. The lecturer spoke about parents and children having a different **value system.** What other systems can you think of?

3. **Co-workers** are people who work together. What other words can you think of which begin with *co-*? What does each one mean?

## Writing It Down

    Taking notes is a quick way to write down information. It is important because it helps us to remember the main ideas in a lecture. Read the summary of the mini-lecture. Decide which words are the most important. (The sentence has eight important words.) Cross out the words that are not important. Discuss your answers.

*There are two kinds of situational stress: the kind of stress that comes from the things around you and the kind of stress that comes from the people around you. (8)*

    There are many different ways to take notes. Here is one way. One blank means one word. Write the important words in the blanks.

_____  _____  _____  _____ :

     —_____   _____

     —_____   _____

 Listen to the mini-lecture one more time. Look at the notes while listening.

# SECTION B

## Before You Listen

### Spelling It Out

Read the following definitions of some words from the mini-lecture. Listen to the words that match the definition. Write down the spelling for each word.

1. _ _ _ _ _ : very good

2. _ _ _ _ _ _ _ : making a loud noise

3. _ _ _ _ _ _ _ _ _ : know and understand

4. _ _ _ _ _ _ _ _ _ : exactly

5. _ _ _ _ _   _ _

   _ _ _ _ _ : something to be proud of

Now practice saying the words.

## As You Listen

 **Checking It Off**

Look at the vocabulary list on page 16. Listen to the mini-lecture. <u>Circle</u> the words that you hear. Discuss your answers with your classmates.

### Zeroing In: Main Idea

This mini-lecture has one main idea. Read the following sentences. Put an X in front of the most important point. Discuss your choice.

_____ 1. Situational stress is the most common type of stress that we have in our lives.

_____ 2. Examples of physical stress include noise pollution and crowding.

_____ 3. Having some kind of stress is very common.

_____ 4. Stress caused by the physical and social environments are the two types of situational stress.

Look again at the phrases on page 18 that tell you that main ideas or important points will follow. Listen to the mini-lecture again. <u>Circle</u> the phrase that you hear. Discuss your answer.

     Listen to this phrase from the mini-lecture. Answer the following questions. Discuss your answers.

1. What is the most important word? _____

2. Does the speaker say this word:

   quickly          slowly

3. Does the speaker say this word:

   loudly          softly

4. Listen to the mini-lecture again. Does the main idea come at the beginning, the middle, or the end?

# After You Listen

## Practicing New Words

■ The words on the left are from the mini-lecture. Practice saying them. Match the words with their definitions on the right. Discuss your answers.

_____ 1. move on              a. a lot of

_____ 2. type                 b. caused

_____ 3. heavy                c. competition

_____ 4. brought on by        d. doctors, lawyers, teachers, etc.

_____ 5. rivalries            e. go ahead

_____ 6. professional people  f. kind

■ Some of these words are from the mini-lecture. Look at each group, and circle the word or phrase that does not belong. What are the reasons for your answers?

| 1. continue | go back | move on | proceed |
|---|---|---|---|
| 2. easily seen | easily stressed | easily understood | obviously |
| 3. controlled | crowded | managed | regulated |
| 4. calm | irritated | stressed out | upset |
| 5. family around us | friends around us | social environment | things around us |
| 6. actually | in reality | really | usually |

■ Read and discuss the following questions with your classmates.

1. **Noise pollution** was said to be a **prime example** of physical stress. What are prime examples for the following:

   - family-related stress
   - work-related stress
   - teacher/student-related stress

2. You can add *out* to many English verbs to make them mean "completely." Some examples are:

   stressed ──────→ stressed out (completely stressed)

   cleaned ──────→ cleaned out (completely cleaned)

   Can you think of some others?

3. The lecturer used the word **heavy,** meaning "a lot of." It also can mean "weighing a great deal." Look at the following words from the lecture. Think of as many different meanings as you can.

   - taking off
   - landing
   - brought on by

## Writing It Down

Taking notes is a quick way to write down information. It is important because it helps us to remember the main ideas in a lecture. Read the following summary of the mini-lecture. Decide which words are the most important. (The sentence has eight important words.) Cross out the words that are not important. Discuss your answers.

*Stress caused by the physical environment and stress caused by the social environment are the two types of situational stress. (8)*

There are many different ways to take notes. Here is one way. One blank means one word. Write the important words in the blanks.

_____  _____  _____  _____ :

_____  _____

_____  _____

Listen to the mini-lecture one more time. Look at the notes while listening.

## Following Up

1. Go to the library. Look up the section on "stress" in the encyclopedia. List as many ways as you can find to help reduce stress.

2. List the source for your information:

   Name of encyclopedia _____

   Volume number _____   Year _____   Page(s) _____

3. Read the discussion suggestions, and choose one to talk or write about.
   a. What kinds of things make you feel stress? Have these things always bothered you?
   b. When you have feelings of stress, what do you do about it? Where did you learn that? How long have you been doing that?

4. Read the transcripts of both mini-lectures. Highlight the main ideas. Highlight any vocabulary that you do not understand, and find the meanings. Listen to the mini-lectures and follow along with the transcripts.

TODAY'S LECTURE

# Business Ownership

# SECTION A

## Before You Listen

### Getting Set

Who do you think owns this business?
Make a list of all the good points and bad points about owning such a place.

*Advantages*

1.

2.

3.

*Disadvantages*

1.

2.

3.

## Talking It Over

You will hear a mini-lecture about business ownership. Look at the following list of words. Practice saying them. Which words do you think that you will hear? Why? Discuss your answers.

assets ⸝                          money

boss                             operated

capital ⸜                         owner ⸝

corporation                      profits ⸜

employees ·                      proprietor

enterprise                       self-employed

entrepreneur ⸝                   sole proprietorship ⸝

invests                          taxes

## Spelling It Out

Read the following definitions of some words from the mini-lecture. Listen to the words that match the definitions. Write down the spelling for each word.

1. __ __ __ __ __ __ __ __

   __ __ : called

2. __ __ __ __ __ __ : asked for and collected

3. __ __ __ __ __ __ __ __ __ : telling someone else

4. __ __ __ __ __ __ __ __ __ : bring to an end

5. __ __ __ __ __ __ __ __ __ : anybody you owe money to

Now practice saying the words.

# As You Listen

 **Checking It Off**

Look at the vocabulary list above. Listen to the mini-lecture. <u>Underline</u> the words that you hear. Discuss your choices.

## Zeroing In: Main Idea

This mini-lecture has one main idea. Read the following sentences. Put an X in front of the most important point. Discuss your choice.

_____ 1. The sole proprietorship is the oldest and most common form of business.

_____ 2. A sole proprietor must pay payroll taxes, income taxes, and property taxes.

_____ 3. In order for a sole proprietor to be successful, that person must be knowledgeable about many things.

__X__ 4. A sole proprietorship is a business which is owned and operated by one person for profit.

Look at the following phrases. They tell you that main ideas or important points will follow. Listen to the mini-lecture again. <u>Underline</u> the phrase that you hear. Discuss your answers.

1. I want to make one impression on you and that is . . .

2. I want you to remember this . . .

3. The topic for today's lesson is . . .

Listen to this phrase from the mini-lecture. Answer the following questions. Discuss your answers.

1. What is the most important word? _____ this _____

2. Does the speaker say this word:

   quickly        slowly  ~

3. Does the speaker say this word:

   loudly  ⌣        softly

4. Listen to the mini-lecture again. Does the main idea come at the beginning, the middle, or the end? ⌣

# After You Listen

## Practicing New Words

■ The words on the left are from the mini-lecture. Practice saying them. Match the words with their definitions on the right. Discuss your answers.

| | | |
|---|---|---|
| _____ 1. fees | a. | begin |
| _____ 2. clients | b. | customers |
| _____ 3. initiate | c. | difference |
| _____ 4. in reverse | d. | knowledge |
| _____ 5. dispersed | e. | money and belongings |
| _____ 6. shingle | f. | money to be paid |
| _____ 7. distinction | g. | not enough |
| _____ 8. insufficient | h. | sign |
| _____ 9. wealth | i. | spent |
| _____ 10. expertise | j. | the other way |

■ Practice saying these words from the lecture. Some are nouns and some are adjectives.

| *Nouns* | *Adjectives* |
|---|---|
| 1. capital | capitalistic |
| 2. profit | profitable |
| 3. information | informational |
| 4. wealth | wealthy |
| 5. knowledge | knowledgeable |

■ Read the following sentences. Write the correct form of the word in the blank. Words from number one on the list go in sentence number one, words from number two on the list go in sentence number two, and so forth. Circle whether the word is a noun or an adjective.

1. a. In the United States there is a _____ form of government.

   noun      adjective

   b. The economics professor explained the importance of

   _____ for starting up a business.   noun      adjective

2. a. Businesses are started so their owners can make a _____ .

      noun    adjective

  b. The teacher lectured on the ten most _____ companies in

      the country.  noun    adjective

3. a. An _____ meeting will be held after class.

      noun    adjective

  b. Pass this _____ on to all your classmates.

      noun    adjective

4. a. A person's _____ includes both money and belongings.

      noun    adjective

  b. We will study the _____ industrialized nations of the

      West next semester.  noun    adjective

5. a. I don't have a great deal of _____ about business and

      economics.  noun    adjective

  b. She was one of the most _____ persons in the study

      group.  noun    adjective

■ Read and discuss the following questions with your classmates.

1. There are hundreds of two-word verbs in English. Some found in the mini-lecture include:

set up      = organize
paid off     = paid completely
taken down = pulled down
hung out   = displayed
draw upon  = take or use as a source

How many others can you think of? What are their meanings?

*Two-Word Verbs*                *Meanings*

a.

b.

c.

d.

e.

2. You can add *dis-* to many English words to make them mean "the opposite." Some examples are:

advantages ⟶ disadvantages

allow ⟶ disallow

obey ⟶ disobey

Can you think of some others?

3. The lecturer mentioned three kinds of taxes: payroll, income, and property taxes. There are many others. Can you name them?

## Writing It Down

Taking notes is a quick way to write down information. It is important because it helps us to remember the main ideas in a lecture. Read the summary of the mini-lecture. Decide which words are the most important. (The sentence has 12 important words.) Cross out the words that are not important. Discuss your answers.

*The definition of a sole proprietorship is that it is a business belonging to and run by one person for the purpose of making money. (12)*

There are many different ways to take notes. Here is one way. One blank means one word. Write the important words in the blanks.

 Listen to the mini-lecture one more time. Look at the notes while listening.

# SECTION B

## Before You Listen

### Spelling It Out

Read the following definitions of some words from the mini-lecture. Listen to the words that match the definition. Write down the spelling for each word.

1. _ _ _ _ _ _ _ _ _ _ : thought of

2. _ _ _ _ _ _ _ : talk to

3. _ _ _ _ _ _ _ _ _ _ _ _ : kept secret

4. _ _ _ _ _ _ _ _ _ : reason for doing something

5. _ _   _ _ _ _
   _ _ _ : by yourself

Now practice saying the words.

## As You Listen

 **Checking It Off**

Look at the vocabulary list on page 27. Listen to the mini-lecture. Circle the words that you hear. Discuss your answers with your classmates.

### Zeroing In: Main Idea

This mini-lecture has one main idea. Read the following sentences. Put an X in front of the most important point. Discuss your choice.

_____ 1. A business that is owned and operated by one person for profit is called a sole proprietorship.

_____ 2. A sole proprietor is considered self-employed.

_____ 3. Sole proprietorships are easy to organize.

_____ 4. People enjoy being their own bosses rather than working for someone else.

Look again at the phrases on page 28 that tell you that main ideas or important points will follow. Listen to the mini-lecture again. Circle the phrase that you hear. Discuss your answer.

 Listen to this phrase from the mini-lecture. Answer the following questions. Discuss your answers.

1. What is the most important word? _____

2. Does the speaker say this word:

   quickly          slowly

3. Does the speaker say this word:

   loudly          softly

4. Listen to the mini-lecture again. Does the main idea come at the beginning, the middle, or the end?

# After You Listen

## Practicing New Words

■ The words on the left are from the mini-lecture. Practice saying them. Match the words with their definitions on the right. Discuss your answers.

_____ 1. within the limits          a. ability to do what you want

_____ 2. freedom of action          b. great

_____ 3. methods                    c. that which is allowed

_____ 4. high                       d. ways to do something

_____ 5. put in                     e. work

■ Some of these words are from the mini-lecture. Look at each group, and circle the word or phrase that does not belong. What are the reasons for your answers?

| 1. subject | summary | theme | topic |
|---|---|---|---|
| 2. number | one | single | sole |
| 3. leadership | ownership | possession | proprietorship |
| 4. defined | managed | operated | run by |
| 5. be employed | consult | punch clocks | work |
| 6. building | business | company | corporation |

■ Read and discuss the following questions with your classmates.

1. The lecturer said that there is a certain **satisfaction** in being your own boss. What kinds of things give you satisfaction? Make a list.

2. The lecturer said that sole proprietorships were **simple to organize.** What other kinds of things are also simple to organize? Why?

3. A common ending in English used to make nouns is *-ship*, as in the following:

proprietor ⟶ proprietorship
scholar     ⟶ scholarship
friend      ⟶ friendship

Can you think of some others?

## Writing It Down

Taking notes is a quick way to write down information. It is important because it helps us to remember the main ideas in a lecture. Read the following summary of the mini-lecture. Decide which words are the most important. (The sentence has 10 important words.) Cross out the words that are not important. Discuss your answers.

*One can define a sole proprietorship as a business that is owned and operated by a single individual to make money. (10)*

There are many different ways to take notes. Here is one way. One blank means one word. Write the important words in the blanks.

_____  _____  — _____
↓

_____ _____ _____  _____
↓

_____ _____ _____

 Listen to the mini-lecture one more time. Look at the notes while listening.

## Following Up

1. Go to the library. Look up "business" in the encyclopedia. What are the three main types of business ownership in the United States? How many are there?

   *Types of Business Ownership*                               *Number*

   a. sole proprietorship

   b.

   c.

2. List the source for your information:

   Name of encyclopedia _____

   Volume number _____   Year _____   Page(s) _____

3. Read the discussion suggestions, and choose one to talk or write about.
   a. Have you ever had your own business? What kind was it? Where did the capital come from to start the business?
   b. Have you ever known anybody to lose their business? What happened?

4. Read the transcripts of both mini-lectures. Highlight the main ideas. Highlight any vocabulary that you do not understand, and find the meanings. Listen to the mini-lectures and follow along with the transcripts.

TODAY'S LECTURE

Global Warming

# SECTION A

## Before You Listen

### Getting Set

Look at the activities above. How does each one make the earth a warmer place? Is that good or bad?

## Talking It Over

You will hear a mini-lecture about global warming. Look at the following list of words. Practice saying them. Which words do you think that you will hear? Why? Discuss your answers.

| | | | |
|---|---|---|---|
| atmosphere | flooding | increasing | planet |
| burning | forests | Industrial Revolution | pollution |
| carbon dioxide | greenhouse effect | melting | smog |
| deforestation | heat | methane | temperature |

## Spelling It Out

Read the following definitions of some words from the mini-lecture. Listen to the words that match the definitions. Write down the spelling for each word.

1. __ __ __ __ __ __ __ : argued

2. __ __ __ __ __ __ __ : unproved idea

3. __ __ __ __ __ __ __ __ __ __ __ __ : not able to be lived in

4. __ __ __ __ __ __ __ __ : cause for something being wrong

5. __ __ __ __ __ __ __ __ __ __ : mostly

Now practice saying the words.

# As You Listen

 **Checking It Off**

Look at the vocabulary list above. Listen to the mini-lecture. <u>Underline</u> the words that you hear. Discuss your choices.

## Zeroing In: Main Idea

This mini-lecture has one main idea. Read the following sentences. Put an X in front of the most important point. Discuss your choice.

_____ 1. Earth Day is a good time to talk about scientific issues which have significance for the whole world.

_____ 2. People are concerned about carbon dioxide and methane increasing in the atmosphere.

_____ 3. When the temperature on earth rises, there will be floods causing great damage.

_____ 4. Carbon dioxide is caused by pollution from industry and automobiles.

Look at the following phrases. They tell you that main ideas or important points will follow. Listen to the mini-lecture again. <u>Underline</u> the phrase that you hear. Discuss your answers.

1. I want to make one impression on you and that is . . .
2. Our subject today is . . .
3. What I'd like to talk about today is . . .

Listen to this phrase from the mini-lecture. Answer the following questions. Discuss your answers.

1. What is the most important word? _____
2. Does the speaker say this word:

   quickly       slowly

3. Does the speaker say this word:

   loudly       softly

4. Listen to the mini-lecture again. Does the main idea come at the beginning, the middle, or the end?

# After You Listen

## Practicing New Words

■ The words on the left are from the mini-lecture. Practice saying them. Match the words with their definitions on the right. Discuss your answers.

| | |
|---|---|
| _____ 1. issue | a. description |
| _____ 2. aware | b. fields |
| _____ 3. concern | c. holding back |
| _____ 4. predicts | d. important point |
| _____ 5. trapping | e. known |
| _____ 6. scenario | f. send out |
| _____ 7. paddies | g. tells the future |
| _____ 8. emit | h. worry |

■ Practice saying these words from the lecture. Some are nouns and some are verbs.

| *Nouns* | *Verbs* |
|---------|---------|
| 1. emission | emit |
| 2. prediction | predict |
| 3. contribution | contribute |
| 4. creation | create |
| 5. pollution | pollute |

■ Read the following sentences. Write the correct form of the word in the blank. Words from number one on the list go in sentence number one, words from number two on the list go in sentence number two, and so forth. Circle whether the word is a noun or a verb.

1. a. All automobiles _____ carbon dioxide into the

   atmosphere.   noun   verb

   b. An _____ of carbon dioxide occurs every time you start

   the car.   noun   verb

2. a. I _____ that the earth will experience great floods.

   noun   verb

   b. What is your _____ for the future of the planet?

   noun   verb

3. a. Her _____ to the class discussion helped everyone

   understand.   noun   verb

   b. Let me _____ this piece of information.   noun   verb

4. a. A good instructor tries to _____ a pleasant study

   atmosphere for students.   noun   verb

   b. The _____ of instructional materials for the classroom

   takes a long time.   noun   verb

5. a. Burning coal adds to the _____ in the air.   noun   verb

   b. If we continue to _____ our environment, global warming

   will increase.   noun   verb

■ Read and discuss the following questions with your classmates.

1. The lecturer said that **chlorofluorocarbons** are known as **CFC's.** CFC is an abbreviation, a short way to say something which is longer. How many abbreviations can you think of? Now look at the "Writing It Down" sections of Units 1, 2, and 3. Change the words in your notes to abbreviations.

2. You can add *-al* or *-ial* to many English words to make them adjectives or nouns. Some examples are:

   industry ————> industrial (adjective)

   arrive   ————> arrival (noun)

   Can you think of some others?

3. The lecturer spoke about **chemical** and **biological processes.** What other processes can you think of?

## Writing It Down

Taking notes is a quick way to write down information. It is important because it helps us to remember the main ideas in a lecture. Read the summary of the mini-lecture. Decide which words are the most important. (The sentence has seven important words.) Cross out the words that are not important. Discuss your answers.

There is great concern today for the ever-increasing amounts of carbon dioxide and methane in the atmosphere. (7)

There are many different ways to take notes. Here is one way. One blank means one word. Write the important words in the blanks. USE ABBREVIATIONS AND/OR SYMBOLS IF YOU CAN.

_____ _____ _____ _____ / _____

_____ _____

Listen to the mini-lecture one more time. Look at the notes while listening.

# SECTION B

## Before You Listen

### Spelling It Out

Read the following definitions of some words from the mini-lecture. Listen to the words that match the definition. Write down the spelling fc each word.

1. _ _ _ _ _ _ _ _ _ _ : something to be remembered

2. _ _ _ _ _ _ _ _ : takes in

3. _ _ _ _ _ : average

4. _ _ _ _ _ : quick

5. _ _ _   _ _ : because of

Now practice saying the words.

## As You Listen

 **Checking It Off**

Look at the vocabulary list on page 39. Listen to the mini-lecture. Circle the words that you hear. Discuss your answers with your class-mates.

### Zeroing In: Main Idea

This mini-lecture has one main idea. Read the following sentences. Put an X in front of the most important point. Discuss your choice.

_____ 1. People are worried about the increasing amounts of carbon dioxide and methane in the air.

_____ 2. Carbon dioxide and methane gas are called greenhouse gases.

_____ 3. The temperature of the earth has risen ever since the late 1800s.

_____ 4. In 1957 the amount of carbon dioxide in the atmosphere was 315 parts per million.

Look again at the phrases on page 40 that tell you that main ideas or important points will follow. Listen to the mini-lecture again. <u>Circle</u> the phrase that you hear. Discuss your answer.

     Listen to this phrase from the mini-lecture. Answer the following questions. Discuss your answers.

1. What is the most important word? _____

2. Does the speaker say this word:

   quickly          slowly

3. Does the speaker say this word:

   loudly          softly

4. Listen to the mini-lecture again. Does the main idea come at the beginning, the middle, or the end?

# After You Listen

### Practicing New Words

■ The words on the left are from the mini-lecture. Practice saying them. Match the words with their definitions on the right. Discuss your answers.

_____ 1. contribute          a.  add to

_____ 2. solar radiation     b.  heat from the sun

_____ 3. surface             c.  including everything

_____ 4. reflects            d.  not enough

_____ 5. mentioned           e.  outer part

_____ 6. overall             f.  spoke about

_____ 7. lack of             g.  throws back

■ Some of these words are from the mini-lecture. Look at each group, and circle the word or phrase that does not belong. What are the reasons for your answers?

| | | | |
|---|---|---|---|
| 1. concern | control | uneasiness | worry |
| 2. absorbs | lets in | reflects | takes in |
| 3. mentioned | spoke about | talked about | wrote about |
| 4. absorbs | escapes | gets away | leaves |
| 5. keeping track of | listening to | recording | writing down |
| 6. gradually | regularly | systematically | thoroughly |
| 7. a lot of | lack of | lots of | plenty of |
| 8. average | in between | in the extreme | mean |

■ Read and discuss the following questions with your classmates.

1. There are many words in English which can be both nouns and verbs. Some examples are:

   concern ——————> There is great **concern** today. (noun)
   It does **concern** scientists. (verb)

   name ——————> What is your **name**? (noun)
   I will **name** the gases. (verb)

   Can you think of some others?

2. You can add *-ly* to adjectives to make them adverbs. Some examples are:

   regular ——————> regularly
   systematical ——————> systematically

   Can you think of some others?

3. The lecturer used the word **mean,** meaning "average." It also can mean "not nice." Look at the following words from the lecture. Think of as many different meanings as you can.
   • impression
   • proof
   • point
   • hold

**Writing It Down**

Taking notes is a quick way to write down information. It is important because it helps us to remember the main ideas in a lecture. Read the following summary of the mini-lecture. Decide which words are the most important. (The sentence has seven important words.) Cross out the words that are not important. Discuss your answers.

*As carbon dioxide and methane increase in the atmosphere, people are becoming worried about the future of our planet. (7)*

There are many different ways to take notes. Here is one way. One blank means one word. Write the important words in the blanks. USE ABBREVIATIONS AND/OR SYMBOLS IF YOU CAN.

———— ———— / ———— ———— ——> ———— ————

———————

 Listen to the mini-lecture one more time. Look at the notes while listening.

**Following Up**

1. Go to the library. Look up "sun" or "climate" or "greenhouse effect" in the encyclopedia. How is the greenhouse effect explained? Copy a simple explanation.
Explanation of the greenhouse effect:

_____

_____

_____

_____

_____

2. If there is an illustration showing the greenhouse effect, make a Xerox copy and bring it to class.

3. List the source for your information:

Name of encyclopedia _____

Volume number _____   Year _____   Page(s) _____

4. Read the discussion suggestions, and choose one to talk or write about.
   a. Make a list of things you can do as a single individual to keep the earth from becoming warmer. Which ones are the most important?
   b. Earth Day began more than twenty years ago. What is it? How do people observe the day in your community?

5. Read the transcripts of both mini-lectures. Highlight the main ideas. Highlight any vocabulary that you do not understand, and find the meanings. Listen to the mini-lectures and follow along with the transcripts.

TODAY'S LECTURE

Exercise

# SECTION A

## Before You Listen

### Getting Set

Do you do any of these activities? Which one is best? Why?

## Talking It Over

You will hear a mini-lecture about exercise. Look at the following list of words. Practice saying them. Which words do you think that you will hear? Why? Discuss your answers.

| | | |
|---|---|---|
| blood pressure | glucose | physicians |
| bloodstream | health | prescription |
| calories | heart | regimen |
| cholesterol profile | insulin | walking |
| diabetes | medications | weight |
| doctor | medicines | |

## Spelling It Out

Read the following definitions of some words from the mini-lecture. Listen to the words that match the definitions. Write down the spelling for each word.

1. — — — — — — —

    — — — — — — — : organization for doctors

2. — — — — — — — — : talking about

3. — — — — — — — — — : says

4. — — — — — : quick

5. — — — — : danger

Now practice saying the words.

# As You Listen

 **Checking It Off**

Look at the vocabulary list above. Listen to the mini-lecture. <u>Underline</u> the words that you hear. Discuss your choices.

## Zeroing In: Main Idea

This mini-lecture has one main idea. Read the following sentences. Put an X in front of the most important point. Discuss your choice.

_____ 1. The largest medical group in the United States is the American College of Physicians.

_____ 2. There are many health advantages for an individual who does walking.

_____ 3. Chances of a heart attack are decreased with walking.

_____ 4. Exercise allows the body to better control the blood sugar level.

Look at the following phrases. They tell you that main ideas or important points will follow. Listen to the mini-lecture again. Underline the phrase that you hear. Discuss your answers.

1. And so we can conclude that . . .
2. Today, I'll be covering . . .
3. What I want you to remember is . . .

Listen to this phrase from the mini-lecture. Answer the following questions. Discuss your answers.

1. What is the most important word? _____
2. Does the speaker say this word:

   quickly        slowly
3. Does the speaker say this word:

   loudly         softly
4. Listen to the mini-lecture again. Does the main idea come at the beginning, the middle, or the end?

# After You Listen

## Practicing New Words

■ The words on the left are from the mini-lecture. Practice saying them. Match the words with their definitions on the right. Discuss your answers.

| | | | |
|---|---|---|---|
| —— | 1. go on | a. | continue |
| —— | 2. provides | b. | gives |
| —— | 3. benefits | c. | good effects |
| —— | 4. research | d. | join together |
| —— | 5. significantly | e. | kept away from |
| —— | 6. associated with | f. | meaningfully |
| —— | 7. avoided | g. | related to |
| —— | 8. burn | h. | study |
| —— | 9. couple . . . with | i. | too much |
| —— | 10. excess | j. | use |

■ Practice saying these words from the mini-lecture. Some are adjectives. Some are adverbs.

| *Adjectives* | *Adverbs* |
|---|---|
| 1. absolute | absolutely |
| 2. medical | medically |
| 3. brisk | briskly |
| 4. obvious | obviously |
| 5. significant | significantly |
| 6. sensitive | sensitively |
| 7. natural | naturally |

■ Read the following sentences. Write the correct form of the word in the blank. Words from number one on the list go in sentence number one, words from number two on the list go in sentence number two, and so forth. Circle whether the word is an adjective or an adverb.

1. a. That exercise lowers the risk of heart disease is an _____ fact.   adjective      adverb

   b. The professor believed that she was _____ right.

   adjective      adverb

2. a. _____ speaking, walking also changes your cholesterol profile.   adjective     adverb

   b. Some students will go to _____ school.
      adjective     adverb

3. a. Everyone should do _____ walking three times a week.
      adjective     adverb

   b. Walking _____ every other day is a good idea.
      adjective     adverb

4. a. Regular exercise promotes _____ health benefits.
      adjective     adverb

   b. You _____ do not do enough exercise.
      adjective     adverb

5. a. A _____ way to control high blood pressure is to get more exercise.   adjective     adverb

   b. Chances of a heart attack are _____ decreased with walking.   adjective     adverb

6. a. A good physician deals with patients _____ .
      adjective     adverb

   b. Exercise and weight loss make the body more _____ to levels of insulin.   adjective     adverb

7. a. Insulin is _____ released into the bloodstream.
      adjective     adverb

   b. The most _____ way to improve your health is by getting exercise.   adjective     adverb

■ Read and discuss the following questions with your classmates.

1. The lecturer spoke about the American College of Physicians as being the largest medical **society** in the U.S. What other societies can you think of?

2. The lecturer said that following a **regimen** of walking three times a week provided great health benefits. What kinds of regimens do you follow? Why?

3. The lecturer mentioned the medications which lower blood pressure often have **side effects.** What kinds of side effects have you had when taking medicine?

**Writing It Down**

Taking notes is a quick way to write down information. It is important because it helps us to remember the main ideas in a lecture. Read the summary of the mini-lecture. Decide which words are the most important. (The sentence has four important words.) Cross out the words that are not important. Discuss your answers.

*Walking provides great health benefits to the individual. (4)*

There are many different ways to take notes. Here is one way. One blank means one word. Write the important words in the blanks. USE ABBREVIATIONS AND/OR SYMBOLS IF YOU CAN.

_____ ⟶ _____   _____   _____

 Listen to the mini-lecture one more time. Look at the notes while listening.

# SECTION B

## Before You Listen

**Spelling It Out**

Read the following definitions of some words from the mini-lecture. Listen to the words that match the definition. Write down the spelling for each word.

1. _ _ _ _ _ _ _ _ :

   _ _   _ _ : thought to be

2. _ _ _ _ _ _ _ _ : go for information

3. _ _ _ _ _ _ _ _ : completely

4. _ _ _ _ _ _ _ _ _ _ : illness or injury

5. _ _ _ _ _ _ _ _ _ _ _ _ _ : about

Now practice saying the words.

## As You Listen

 **Checking It Off**

Look at the vocabulary list on page 49. Listen to the mini-lecture. <u>Circle</u> the words that you hear. Discuss your answers with your classmates.

### Zeroing In: Main Idea

This mini-lecture has one main idea. Read the following sentences. Put an X in front of the most important point. Discuss your choice.

_____ 1. Walking is thought to be one of the best ways to make your health better.

_____ 2. If you are in good health, there is no need to consult a doctor before walking.

_____ 3. Walking can help control high blood pressure.

_____ 4. It is recommended that you walk twenty minutes a day, three times a week.

Look again at the phrases on page 50 that tell you that main ideas or important points will follow. Listen to the mini-lecture again. Circle the phrase that you hear. Discuss your answer.

Listen to this phrase from the mini-lecture. Answer the following questions. Discuss your answers.

1. What is the most important word? _____

2. Does the speaker say this word:

   quickly          slowly

3. Does the speaker say this word:

   loudly          softly

4. Listen to the mini-lecture again. Does the main idea come at the beginning, the middle, or the end?

# After You Listen

### Practicing New Words

■ The words on the left are from the mini-lecture. Practice saying them. Match the words with their definitions on the right. Discuss your answers.

_____ 1. average             a. change

_____ 2. minimum             b. least

_____ 3. alter               c. partly

_____ 4. to a certain extent d. usual/ordinary

■ Some of these words are from the mini-lecture. Look at each group, and circle the word or phrase that does not belong. What are the reasons for your answers?

1. investigation     research        study          writing
2. cholesterol       medication      medicine       prescription
3. consult           pay             see            talk to
4. assuming          considering     remembering    supposing
5. least             maximum         minimum        smallest
6. description       prescription    profile        summary

■ Read and discuss the following questions with your classmates.

1. You can add *dis-* to many English words to make them mean "the opposite of." Some examples are:

   ability ———————> disability

   approve ———————> disapprove

   Can you think of some others?

2. The lecturer said that walking is **supposed to be** one of the best things someone can do to improve health. What other things are supposed to be good for your health? How do you know?

3. Diabetes can be controlled **to a certain extent** by exercise. What can be controlled to a certain extent by not smoking? By not drinking alcohol? By avoiding the sun between 10:00 and 2:00? By reading every day for an hour?

## Writing It Down

Taking notes is a quick way to write down information. It is important because it helps us to remember the main ideas in a lecture. Read the following summary of the mini-lecture. Decide which words are the most important. (The sentence has four important words.) Cross out the words that are not important. Discuss your answers.

*One of the best things a person can do to improve his or her health is to do a lot of walking. (4)*

There are many different ways to take notes. Here is one way. One blank means one word. Write the important words in the blanks. USE ABBREVIATIONS AND/OR SYMBOLS IF YOU CAN.

——————  ——————  ——————  —→  ——————

 Listen to the mini-lecture one more time. Look at the notes while listening.

## Following Up

1. Go to the library. Look up "exercise" or "physical fitness" in the encyclopedia. What does the President's Council on Physical Fitness and Sports or the American Medical Association say about the subject? Copy some of their comments:

   _____

   _____

   _____

   _____

   _____

2. If you can find any illustrations about exercise and health, make photocopies and bring them to class.

3. List the source for your information:

   Name of encyclopedia _____

   Volume number _____ Year _____ Page(s) _____

4. Read the discussion suggestions, and choose one to talk or write about.
   a. What kinds of exercise do you do? How often? How long have you been exercising?
   b. Are physical education classes part of the school curriculum in your country? How important do you think they are? Why?

5. Read the transcripts of both mini-lectures. Highlight the main ideas. Highlight any vocabulary that you do not understand, and find the meanings. Listen to the mini-lectures and follow along with the transcripts.

TODAY'S LECTURE

Bridges

# SECTION A

## Before You Listen

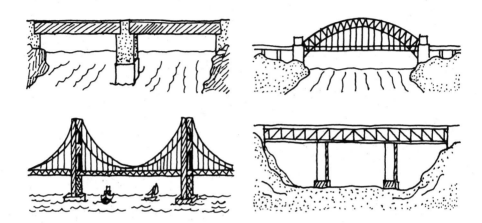

### Getting Set

Look at these four kinds of bridges. Which ones have you seen in real life before? Where? Which one do you think is *not* found in nature? Why?

### Talking It Over

You will hear a mini-lecture about bridges. Look at the following list of words. Practice saying them. Which words do you think that you will hear? Why? Discuss your answers.

| | | |
|---|---|---|
| access | in nature | stream |
| arch | in touch | strength |
| beam | invention | suspension |
| braces | parallel | tree |
| chasm | railings | truss |
| construction | river | unstable |
| horizontal | spanning | vines |
| | | water |

## Spelling It Out

Read the following definitions of some words from the mini-lecture. Listen to the words that match the definitions. Write down the spelling for each word.

1. __ __ __ __ __ __ __ __ __ __ __

   __ __ __ __ __ __ __ __ __ __ : closely connected

2. __ __ __ __ __ __ __ __ __ __ __ : life, society, culture

3. __ __ __ __ __ __

   __ __ __ __ __ __ __ : creatures which live together in groups, not
   alone

4. __ __ __ __ __ __ __ __ __ : something that is wanted

5. __ __ __ __ __ __ __ __   __ __ : come to mind

Now practice saying the words.

# As You Listen

 **Checking It Off**

Look at the vocabulary list on page 58. Listen to the mini-lecture. <u>Underline</u> the words that you hear. Discuss your choices.

## Zeroing In: Main Idea

This mini-lecture has one main idea. Read the following sentences. Put an X in front of the most important point. Discuss your choice.

_____ 1. Bridges are interesting because they are part of human life.

_____ 2. Bridges are needed by human beings because people are social animals.

_____ 3. There are four kinds of bridges: beam, arch, suspension, and truss.

_____ 4. The truss bridge is not found in nature.

 Look at the following phrases. They tell you that main ideas or important points will follow. Listen to the mini-lecture again. <u>Underline</u> the phrase that you hear. Discuss your answers.

1. And today I'll be covering . . .

2. Our subject today is . . .

3. To summarize, then, . . .

Listen to this phrase from the mini-lecture. Important words are said slowly and loudly. Answer the following questions. Discuss your answers.

1. What is the most important word? _____

2. Listen to the mini-lecture again. Does the main idea come at the beginning, the middle, or the end?

# After You Listen

### Practicing New Words

■ The words on the left are from the mini-lecture. Practice saying them. Match the words with their definitions on the right. Discuss your answers.

| | | |
|---|---|---|
| _____ 1. fell | a. | beginnings |
| _____ 2. illusion | b. | cut down |
| _____ 3. coastlines | c. | difficult to understand |
| _____ 4. wear away | d. | false understanding of what one sees |
| _____ 5. origin | e. | hot weather |
| _____ 6. tropical | f. | lands touching the ocean |
| _____ 7. enormously | g. | name of female storybook character |
| _____ 8. Tarzan | h. | name of male storybook character |
| _____ 9. Jane | i. | slowly break to pieces |
| _____ 10. complex | j. | very large |

■ Practice saying these words from the lecture. Some are nouns. Some are adjectives.

| *Nouns* | *Adjectives* |
|---|---|
| 1. society | social |
| 2. desire | desirable |
| 3. nature | natural |
| 4. access | accessible |
| 5. convenience | convenient |
| 6. horizon | horizontal |
| 7. origin | original |
| 8. tropics | tropical |
| 9. complexities | complex |

■ Read the following sentences. Write the correct form of the word in the blank. Words from number one on the list go in sentence number one, words from number two on the list go in sentence number two, and so forth. Circle whether the word is a noun or an adjective.

1. a. Human beings are _____ animals.  noun    adjective

   b. Sociology is the study of _____.  noun    adjective

2. a. My study group has a great _____ to get the best grade on the exam.  noun    adjective

   b. Reading is a _____ way to learn new vocabulary.
      noun    adjective

3. a. Getting together with other people is a _____ thing to do.
      noun    adjective

   b. One can find three different kinds of bridges in _____ .
      noun    adjective

4. a. How _____ is that place from here?  noun    adjective

   b. What _____ is there to the other side of the stream?
      noun    adjective

5. a. An automobile is an expensive _____ .  noun    adjective

   b. Taking a taxi is the most _____ way to get there.
      noun    adjective

6. a. Can you see anything on the _____ ?  noun    adjective

   b. The bottom part of an arch bridge is _____ .
      noun    adjective

7. a. The instructor wants our themes to be as _____ as possible.  noun    adjective

   b. What is the _____ of the suspension bridge?
      noun    adjective

8. a. Have you ever been to the _____ ?  noun    adjective

   b. Vines are most often found in _____ places.
      noun    adjective

9. a. I don't understand the _____ of the situation.

   noun     adjective

   b. The teacher presented us with a _____ set of problems.

   noun     adjective

■ Read and discuss the following questions with your classmates.

1. **Interspaced** means "spaced between." How many other words can you think of that begin with *inter-*? What does each one mean?

2. The lecturer mentioned a proverb (or wise saying) "The grass is greener on the other side," meaning "Things seem to be better in other places." Do you know any proverbs or wise sayings? What do they mean?

3. The lecturer said that human beings are **social animals.** Can you think of any others?

## Writing It Down

Taking notes is a quick way to write down information. It is important because it helps us to remember the main ideas in a lecture. Read the summary of the mini-lecture. Decide which words are the most important. (The sentence has six important words.) Cross out the words that are not important. Discuss your answers.

*There are four completely different kinds of bridges: the beam, the arch, the suspension, and the truss. (6)*

There are many different ways to take notes. Here is one way. One blank means one word. Write the important words in the blanks. USE ABBREVIATIONS AND/OR SYMBOLS IF YOU CAN.

_____   _____

1. _____

2. _____

3. _____

4. _____

 Listen to the mini-lecture one more time. Look at the notes while listening.

# SECTION B

## Before You Listen

### Spelling It Out

Read the following definitions of some words from the mini-lecture. Listen to the words that match the definition. Write down the spelling for each word.

1. __ __

__ __ __ __ __ __ __ __ __ __

__ __ __ __ __ : thousands of years ago

2. __ __ __ __ __ __ __ __ : copied

3. __ __ __ __ __ __ __ __ __ __ __ : wonderful to see

4. __ __ __ __ __ __ __ : wearing away

5. __ __ __ __ __ __ __ : long lasting

Now practice saying the words.

## As You Listen

 **Checking It Off**

Look at the vocabulary list on page 58. Listen to the mini-lecture. <u>Circle</u> the words that you hear. Discuss your answers with your classmates.

### Zeroing In: Main Idea

This mini-lecture has one main idea. Read the following sentences. Put an X in front of the most important point. Discuss your choice.

_____ 1. The beam, arch, suspension, and truss bridges are four completely different kinds of bridges.

_____ 2. It is interesting that the beam, arch, and suspension bridges are found in nature.

_____ 3. An example of a beam bridge is where a tree has fallen down over a stream.

_____ 4. Truss bridges are made stronger with the use of braces.

Look again at the phrases on page 59 that tell you that main ideas or important points will follow. Listen to the mini-lecture again. <u>Circle</u> the phrase that you hear. Discuss your answer.

 Listen to this phrase from the mini-lecture. Answer the following questions. Discuss your answers.

1. What is the most important word? _____

2. Listen to the mini-lecture again. Does the main idea come at the beginning, the middle, or the end?

# After You Listen

## Practicing New Words

■ The words on the left are from the mini-lecture. Practice saying them. Match the words with their definitions on the right. Discuss your answers.

_____ 1. directly              a. all right

_____ 2. satisfactory          b. be seen

_____ 3. appear                c. developed slowly

_____ 4. evolved               d. made longer

_____ 5. expanded              e. made stronger

_____ 6. imagination           f. power of the mind

_____ 7. strengthened          g. straight

■ Some of these words are from the mini-lecture. Look at each group, and circle the word or phrase that does not belong. What are the reasons for your answers?

| | | | |
|---|---|---|---|
| 1. completely | partly | totally | very |
| 2. copied | imitated | invented | reproduced |
| 3. passing across | passing over | spanning | walking |
| 4. ancient | old | historic | prehistoric |
| 5. breaking down | erosion | expansion | wearing away |
| 6. durable | educated | hard | long lasting |
| 7. admirers | fans | leaders | supporters |
| 8. humankind | mankind | person | the human race |
| 9. arches | braces | supports | trusses |

■ Read and discuss the following questions with your classmates.

1. The lecturer said that man **copied nature's way of spanning a river.** Can you think of other ways that man has copied nature's way of doing something?

2. *Pre-* is added to the beginning of some English words to make them mean "before." Some examples are:

|  |  | *Meaning* |
|---|---|---|
| historic | ⟶ prehistoric | before history; very old |
| war | ⟶ prewar | before a war |
| school | ⟶ preschool | relating to children who are too young to go to school |

   Can you think of some others? What are their meanings?

3. The lecturer said an **educated guess** would be that man made beam bridges by copying what already was seen in nature. Can you make an educated guess about the following question:

   How was fire discovered by prehistoric people?

## Writing It Down

   Taking notes is a quick way to write down information. It is important because it helps us to remember the main ideas in a lecture. Read the following summary of the mini-lecture. Decide which words are the most important. (The sentence has six important words.) Cross out the words that are not important. Discuss your answers.

   *The beam, the arch, the suspension, and the truss are the names of distinctly different bridge forms. (6)*

   There are many different ways to take notes. Here is one way. One blank means one word. Write the important words in the blanks. USE ABBREVIATIONS AND/OR SYMBOLS IF YOU CAN.

 Listen to the mini-lecture one more time. Look at the notes while listening.

**Following Up**

1. Go to the library. Look up the section on "bridges" in the encyclopedia. Find out more about truss bridges. Copy a few words from the encyclopedia that explain truss bridges.

   Truss bridges: _____

   _____

   _____

   _____

   _____

2. Does the encyclopedia have any pictures or diagrams showing different bridge forms? If so, make photocopies and bring them to class.

3. List the sources for your information:

   Name of encyclopedia _____

   Volume number _____ Year _____ Page(s) _____

4. Read the discussion suggestions, and choose one to talk or write about:
   a. How many different kinds of bridges are there in your community? Where are they located?
   b. Do you know the names of any famous bridges? Where are they located? Do you know what kind of bridge each one is?

5. Read the transcripts of both mini-lectures. Highlight the main ideas. Highlight any vocabulary that you do not understand, and find the meanings. Listen to the mini-lectures and follow along with the transcripts.

TODAY'S LECTURE

Computer Bulletin Boards

# SECTION A

## Before You Listen

### Getting Set

Have you ever used a computer? If so, what kinds of things did you do? If not, would you like to learn? Why?

### Talking It Over

You will hear a mini-lecture about computer bulletin boards. Look at the following list of words. Practice saying them. Which words do you think that you will hear? Why? Discuss your answers.

| | | |
|---|---|---|
| caller | exchange | modem |
| communicate | hooked into | operator |
| connects | information | screen |
| correspond | keyboard | telephone |
| electronic | message | typing |

## Spelling It Out

Read the following definitions of some words from the mini-lecture. Listen to the words that match the definitions. Write down the spelling for each word.

1. _ _ _ _ _ _ _ _ : find out

2. _ _ _ _ _ : way or method

3. _ _ _ _ _ -_ _ _ : completely new

4. _ _ _ _ _ : kinds

5. _ _ _ _ _ _ _ _ _ _ : specific

Now practice saying the words.

# As You Listen

 **Checking It Off**

Look at the vocabulary list on page 68. Listen to the mini-lecture. Underline the words that you hear. Discuss your choices.

## Zeroing In: Main Idea

This mini-lecture has one main idea. Read the following sentences. Put an X in front of the most important point. Discuss your choice.

_____ 1. Computer bulletin boards have completely changed the way people exchange information.

_____ 2. There are two kinds of computer bulletin boards: a "read-only" board and a "read-and-write" board.

_____ 3. With computer bulletins, it is possible to communicate with people without seeing them.

_____ 4. Messages can be left on computer bulletin boards for someone who does not have to answer immediately.

 Look at the following phrases. They tell you that main ideas or important points will follow. Listen to the mini-lecture again. Underline the phrase that you hear. Discuss your answers.

1. Could you please remember, then, . . .

2. In conclusion, then, I want you to understand that . . .

3. Let us today examine why . . .

Listen to this phrase from the mini-lecture. Important words are said slowly and loudly. Answer the following questions. Discuss your answers.

1. What is the most important word? _____

2. Listen to the mini-lecture again. Does the main idea come at the beginning, the middle, or the end?

# After You Listen

## Practicing New Words

■ The words on the left are from the mini-lecture. Practice saying them. Match the words with their definitions on the right. Discuss your answers.

_____ 1. revolutionized          a. asked to

_____ 2. invited to              b. answer

_____ 3. respond                 c. completely changed

_____ 4. anonymity               d. let something be done

_____ 5. allowed                 e. limited in freedom

_____ 6. barrier                 f. make known with words

_____ 7. express                 g. not having your name known

_____ 8. tied down               h. regularly

_____ 9. periodically            i. something that controls

_____ 10. globe                  j. world

■ Practice saying these words from the mini-lecture. Some are nouns. Some are verbs.

| *Nouns* | *Verbs* |
|---|---|
| 1. communication | communicate |
| 2. examination | examine |
| 3. revolution | revolutionize |
| 4. information | inform |
| 5. choice | choose |
| 6. invitation | invite |
| 7. response | respond |
| 8. correspondence | correspond |
| 9. protection | protect |
| 10. expression | express |
| 11. collection | collect |
| 12. preference | prefer |

■ Read the following sentences. Write the correct form of the word in the blank. Words from number one on the list go in sentence number one, words from number two on the list go in sentence number two, and so forth. Circle whether the word is a noun or a verb.

1. a. A computer makes it easy to _____ with other people.

   noun     verb

   b. Using a computer bulletin board is a new method of

   _____ .   noun     verb

2. a. Let us _____ why computers have become so popular.

   noun     verb

   b. You will have to study hard to pass the _____ .

   noun     verb

3. a. A _____ is taking place in how people communicate.

   noun     verb

   b. Computers will continue to _____ the way people live.

   noun     verb

4. a. Getting _____ about something is easy at the library.

   noun     verb

   b. You have to _____ yourself about the subject.

   noun     verb

5. a. The _____ is up to the individual.   noun     verb

   b. You have to learn to pick and _____ information.

   noun     verb

6. a. Did you get an _____ to the chancellor's reception?

   noun     verb

   b. She did not _____ them to the dorm party.

   noun     verb

7. a. Let me _____ to you this way.   noun     verb

   b. What was the student's _____ to the question?

   noun     verb

8.  a. Are you going to _____ with the college during the
       summer?   noun      verb

    b. My _____ with the Dean of Students is in the file.
       noun      verb

9.  a. For your own _____ , save that part of the essay.
       noun      verb

    b. The campus police _____ college property.
       noun      verb

10. a. Can you _____ that feeling in another way?
       noun      verb

    b. He offered an _____ of thanks.   noun      verb

11. a. My assignment is to _____ as much information about
       the subject as possible.   noun      verb

    b. You can find that information in the rare book _____ in
       the library.   noun      verb

12. a. I have a _____ for living alone.   noun      verb

    b. Which do you _____ , a single or a double room?
       noun      verb

■ Read and discuss the following questions with your classmates.

1. The lecturer said that computer bulletin boards have **revolutionized**
   the way people exchange information. Can you think of other things
   which have revolutionized the way people do things?

2. *Rewrite* means to "write something again." How many other words
   can you think of that begin with *re-* and mean to "do something
   again?"

3. The lecturer said that bulletin boards for computer users have become
   the **preferred method** of communicating. What is the preferred
   method for the following activities:

   • paying bills
   • transportation (short trips)
   • transportation (long trips)
   • losing weight

## Writing It Down

Taking notes is a quick way to write down information. It is important because it helps us to remember the main ideas in a lecture. Read the summary of the mini-lecture. Decide which words are the most important. (The sentence has seven important words.) Cross out the words that are not important. Discuss your answers.

*Many who use the computer bulletin board system believe they have discovered a form of communication that is revolutionizing the way we exchange information. (7)*

There are many different ways to take notes. Here is one way. One blank means one word. Write the important words in the blanks. USE ABBREVIATIONS AND/OR SYMBOLS IF YOU CAN.

_____  _____  _____ = _____  _____

_____  _____

 Listen to the mini-lecture one more time. Look at the notes while listening.

# SECTION B

# Before You Listen

## Spelling It Out

Read the following definitions of some words from the mini-lecture. Listen to the words that match the definition. Write down the spelling for each word.

1. \_ \_ \_ \_ \_ \_ \_ \_ \_ \_ : people with strong feelings of support

2. \_ \_ \_ \_ : decides on

3. \_ \_ \_  \_ \_ \_ : stop

4. \_ \_ \_ \_ \_ \_ \_ : can be seen

5. \_ \_ \_ \_ \_ \_ : grow larger

Now practice saying the words.

# As You Listen

 **Checking It Off**

Look at the vocabulary list on page 68. Listen to the mini-lecture. Circle the words that you hear. Discuss your answers with your classmates.

## Zeroing In: Main Idea

This mini-lecture has one main idea. Read the following sentences. Put an X in front of the most important point. Discuss your choice.

_____ 1. A computer bulletin board system needs a computer, a telephone, and a modem.

_____ 2. System operators in a computer bulletin board system are called "sysops."

_____ 3. One can watch, listen, and talk back in a computer bulletin board system.

_____ 4. The computer bulletin board system has great possibilities, and it will probably expand greatly.

Look again at the phrases on page 69 that tell you that main ideas or important points will follow. Listen to the mini-lecture again. Circle the phrase that you hear. Discuss your answer.

Listen to this phrase from the mini-lecture. Answer the following questions. Discuss your answers.

1. What is the most important word? _____

2. Listen to the mini-lecture again. Does the main idea come at the beginning, the middle, or the end?

# After You Listen

## Practicing New Words

■ The words on the left are from the mini-lecture. Practice saying them. Match the words with their definitions on the right. Discuss your answers.

_____ 1. requires                a. copy

_____ 2. get into                b. enter

_____ 3. stay on                 c. indecent, offensive language

_____ 4. record                  d. needs

_____ 5. four-letter words       e. remain

■ Some of these words are from the mini-lecture. Look at each group, and circle the word or phrase that does not belong. What are the reasons for your answers?

| | | | |
|---|---|---|---|
| 1. enthusiasts | fans | supporters | users |
| 2. decides | demands | needs | requires |
| 3. changes | connects | hooks | joins |
| 4. decides on | listens to | makes up | sets |
| 5. four-letter words | indecent language | ungrammatical language | vulgar language |

■ Read and discuss the following questions with your classmates.

1. The lecturer said that systems operators are called "sysops." Sysops is a shorter word for a longer word. What shorter words that stand for longer words can you think of?

2. A computer bulletin board system **requires** a computer, a telephone, and a modem. What does each of the following require?
   - getting good grades
   - learning new words
   - writing a composition

## Writing It Down

Taking notes is a quick way to write down information. It is important because it helps us to remember the main ideas in a lecture. Read the following summary of the mini-lecture. Decide which words are the most important. (The sentence has nine important words.) Cross out the words that are not important. Discuss your answers.

*The way information is exchanged is being revolutionized by the computer bulletin board system. (9)*

There are many different ways to take notes. Here is one way. One blank means one word. Write the important words in the blanks. USE ABBREVIATIONS AND/OR SYMBOLS IF YOU CAN.

_____  _____  _____  ⟶  _____

_____  _____  _____  _____  _____

Listen to the mini-lecture one more time. Look at the notes while listening.

## Following Up

1. Go to the library. Look up the section on "computers" in the encyclopedia. What uses of the computer can you find for the following areas? Copy a few for each.

Business/Industry: _____

_____

_____

_____

_____

Government: _____

_____

_____

_____

_____

Education: _____

_____

_____

_____

_____

Home: _____

_____

_____

_____

_____

2. List the sources for your information:

Name of encyclopedia _____

Volume number _____  Year _____  Page(s) _____

3. Read the discussion suggestions, and choose one to talk or write about.
   a. If you know how to use a computer, when did you learn? How
      long did it take? What kinds of things can you do with the
      computer?
   b. If you don't know how to use a computer, why haven't you
      learned? Do you know other people who don't know how? What
      are their reasons for not learning?

4. Read the transcripts of both mini-lectures. Highlight the main ideas.
   Highlight any vocabulary that you do not understand, and find the
   meanings. Listen to the mini-lectures and follow along with the
   transcripts.

TODAY'S LECTURE

Diet

# SECTION A

## Before You Listen

### Getting Set

These people are getting ready to eat dinner.

What are they going to eat?

Did people eat the same kind of food thousands of years ago?

Which food was more popular then?

### Talking It Over

You will hear a mini-lecture about diet. Look at the following list of words. Practice saying them. Which words do you think that you will hear? Why? Discuss your answers.

| | | |
|---|---|---|
| animals | flesh-eater | meat |
| beans | food(s) | nutrition |
| bones | fruit | nuts |
| calories | gnawing | plant(s) |
| carnivorous | grains | roots |
| chewing | hungry | seeds |
| consuming | leaves | teeth |
| dinner | meals | vegetarian |
| eating | | |

## Spelling It Out

Read the following definitions of some words from the mini-lecture. Listen to the words that match the definitions. Write down the spelling for each word.

1. __ __ __ __ __ __ : give the meaning for

2. __ __ __ __ __ __ __

    __ __ __ __   __ __ : reducing the amount

3. __ __ __ __ __ __ __ : plan or set of rules

4. __ __ __ __ __ __ __ __ : rich

5. __ __ __ __ __ __ __ : throw away or get rid of

Now practice saying the words.

# As You Listen

**Checking It Off**

Look at the vocabulary list on page 80. Listen to the mini-lecture. <u>Underline</u> the words that you hear. Discuss your choices.

## Zeroing In: Main Idea

This mini-lecture has one main idea. Read the following sentences. Put an X in front of the most important point. Discuss your choice.

_____ 1. One definition of diet is controlling the amount of food one eats.

_____ 2. Americans eat more meat than any other group.

_____ 3. To make our lives better and longer, we need to eat what prehistoric people ate.

_____ 4. People started to eat meat about one and a half million years ago.

Look at the following phrases. They tell you that main ideas or important points will follow. Listen to the mini-lecture again. <u>Underline</u> the phrase that you hear. Discuss your answers.

1. The important thing to remember is . . .
2. The key point is . . .
3. One could conclude that . . .

Listen to this phrase from the mini-lecture. Answer the following questions. Discuss your answers.

1. What is the most important word? _____
2. Listen to the mini-lecture again. Does the main idea come at the beginning, the middle, or the end?

# After You Listen

## Practicing New Words

■ The words on the left are from the mini-lecture. Practice saying them. Match the words with their definitions on the right. Discuss your answers.

_____ 1. to that effect

_____ 2. maintaining

_____ 3. consists of

_____ 4. voracious

_____ 5. ancestors

_____ 6. mastodons

_____ 7. conventional wisdom

_____ 8. anthropologist

_____ 9. take for granted

_____ 10. fossilized

a. accept as fact without questioning

b. animal/plant of long ago preserved in rock

c. animals looking like elephants that are no longer living

d. belief most people think is true

e. is made up of

f. keeping

g. meaning something similar

h. person who studies human culture

i. relatives who lived long ago

j. wanting large amounts

■ Practice saying these words from the lecture. Some are nouns and some are adjectives.

| Nouns | Adjectives |
|-------|------------|
| 1. diet | dietary |
| 2. definition | definitive |
| 3. variety | various |
| 4. purpose | purposeful |
| 5. nutrition | nutritional |
| 6. affluence | affluent |
| 7. sophistication | sophisticated |
| 8. tradition | traditional |
| 9. ancestor | ancestoral |
| 10. convention | conventional |
| 11. wisdom | wise |
| 12. truth | truthful |
| 13. technology | technological |
| 14. access | accessible |
| 15. fossil | fossilized |

■ Read the following sentences. Write the correct form of the word in the blank. Words from number one on the list go in sentence number one, words from number two on the list go in sentence number two, and so forth. Circle whether the word is a noun or an adjective.

1. a. Americans have a _____ tradition of eating meat.

    noun      adjective

   b. Professor Matthews needs to go on a _____ .

    noun      adjective

2. a. Please give me the _____ for the word "archaeologist."

    noun      adjective

   b. This book contains the _____ study of the American

    diet.   noun      adjective

3. a. It is wise to eat a _____ of food.   noun      adjective

   b. One should have _____ things to eat in one's diet.

    noun      adjective

4. a. One _____ way to review for the test is to look at the lecture notes.   noun     adjective

    b. What is the _____ for making such a difficult assignment?   noun     adjective

5. a. It is important to maintain a balance in the body's _____ . noun     adjective

    b. What is the _____ value of a hamburger? noun     adjective

6. a. People who live in _____ countries eat a lot of meat. noun     adjective

    b. What people eat is determined by a country's _____ . noun     adjective

7. a. How _____ are these language-learning students? noun     adjective

    b. The _____ of the ancient culture surprised the anthropologist.   noun     adjective

8. a. Do you have a dietary _____ in your family? noun     adjective

    b. It is _____ to eat turkey on Thanksgiving. noun     adjective

9. a. Our _____ home was located in the north. noun     adjective

    b. Which _____ came from the Philippines? noun     adjective

10. a. The student followed _____ by typing the homework assignment.   noun     adjective

    b. The teacher follows a _____ method of instruction. noun     adjective

11. a. Does _____ always come with age?   noun     adjective

    b. Many students feel their instructor is a _____ person. noun     adjective

12. a. Be _____ when answering the question.

    noun    adjective

    b. Please tell me the _____ .  noun    adjective

13. a. A teacher must keep up with all the latest _____ .

    noun    adjective

    b. There have been great _____ advances in the twentieth

    century.  noun    adjective

14. a. Computers have given us _____ to more information.

    noun    adjective

    b. Teachers should make themselves _____ to their

    students.  noun    adjective

15. a. Animal bones became _____ .  noun    adjective

    b. Show me an example of a _____ .  noun    adjective

■ Read and discuss the following questions with your classmates.

1. You can add -ist to some English words to make them mean "a person
   who studies, plays or operates something." Some examples are:

   archaeology ————⟶ archaeologist (a person who studies
                                    archaeology)

   anthropology ————⟶ anthropologist (a person who studies
                                      anthropology)

   piano ———————⟶ pianist (a person who plays the piano)

   Can you think of some others?

2. The lecturer said that as countries become more wealthy, their people
   throw off their vegetarian traditions and begin to eat more meat. What
   other **traditions** do people **discard**?

3. The lecturer mentioned **technological advances** today. Can you think
   of some examples?

## Writing It Down

Taking notes is a quick way to write down information. It is important because it helps us to remember the main ideas in a lecture. Read the summary of the mini-lecture. Decide which words are the most important. (The sentence has eight important words.) Cross out the words that are not important. Discuss your answers.

*It is necessary to eat the same things that our ancestors did in order for health to improve and to live longer. (8)*

There are many different ways to take notes. Here is one way. One blank means one word. Write the important words in the blanks. USE ABBREVIATIONS AND/OR SYMBOLS IF YOU CAN.

_____  _____  _____  _____ ⟶ \_\_\_\_\_  _____ /

_____  _____

Listen to the mini-lecture one more time. Look at the notes while listening.

# SECTION B

# Before You Listen

## Spelling It Out

Read the following definitions of some words from the mini-lecture. Listen to the words that match the definition. Write down the spelling for each word.

1. \_\_ \_\_ \_\_ \_\_ \_\_ \_\_ \_\_ \_\_ \_\_ : process of growth or development

2. \_\_ \_\_ \_\_ \_\_ \_\_ \_\_ : take and use as one's own

3. \_\_ \_\_ \_\_ \_\_ \_\_ \_\_ \_\_ \_\_ \_\_ \_\_ : made something seem larger

4. \_\_ \_\_ \_\_ \_\_ \_\_ \_\_ \_\_ : elephant-like animal which is no longer living

5. \_\_ \_\_ \_\_ \_\_ : not mixed

Now practice saying the words.

# As You Listen

 **Checking It Off**

Look at the vocabulary list on page 80. Listen to the mini-lecture. Circle the words that you hear. Discuss your answers with your classmates.

## Zeroing In: Main Idea

This mini-lecture has one main idea. Read the following sentences. Put an X in front of the most important point. Discuss your choice.

_____ 1. If we want to live longer and healthier lives, we must eat how our ancestors did.

_____ 2. Anthropologists used to think early man ate a lot of meat.

_____ 3. People living long ago ate eighty percent plant food.

_____ 4. Scientists observe that the wear patterns on the teeth are identical to those of fruit-eaters.

Look again at the phrases on page 82 that tell you that main ideas or important points will follow. Listen to the mini-lecture again. Circle the phrase that you hear. Discuss your answer.

Listen to this phrase from the mini-lecture. Answer the following questions. Discuss your answers.

1. What is the most important word? _____

2. Listen to the mini-lecture again. Does the main idea come at the beginning, the middle, or the end?

# After You Listen

## Practicing New Words

■ The words on the left are from the mini-lecture. Practice saying them. Match the words with their definitions on the right. Discuss your answers.

| | | |
|---|---|---|
| _____ 1. tribal | a. | correct |
| _____ 2. generation | b. | decide |
| _____ 3. come to the conclusion | c. | goes bad |
| _____ 4. deteriorates | d. | having nothing |
| _____ 5. preserve | e. | keep unchanged |
| _____ 6. empty-handed | f. | modern |
| _____ 7. accurate | g. | people in a group |
| _____ 8. evidence | h. | proof |
| _____ 9. contemporary | i. | solid waste from the body |
| _____ 10. feces | j. | thirty-year period |

■ Some of these words are from the mini-lecture. Look at each group, and circle the word or phrase that does not belong. What are the reasons for your answers?

| | | | |
|---|---|---|---|
| 1. diet | exercise | food | nutrition |
| 2. evolution | development | progression | revolution |
| 3. humankind | human race | individual | mankind |
| 4. adopt | copy | follow | invent |
| 5. ancestors | children | grandparents | great uncles |
| 6. anthropologists | archaeologists | pianists | sociologists |
| 7. elephant | mammoth | mastodon | monkey |
| 8. becomes bad | decays | deteriorates | preserves |
| 9. keep | preserve | stay changed | stay unchanged |
| 10. fact | idea | reality of the matter | truth |
| 11. clubs | guns | spears | sticks |
| 12. collecting | gathering | picking | planting |
| 13. exactly | largely | mostly | predominantly |
| 14. exaggerated | fossilized | preserved | unchanged |
| 15. alike | chemical | identical | similar |
| 16. analysis | conclusion | examination | investigation |

■ Read and discuss the following questions with your classmates.

1. The lecturer spoke about the wear patterns on fossilized teeth. Where else and what other places can you see **wear patterns**?

2. The lecturer explained that a **midden** was the same place where tribal people would eat generation after generation. Think about your own family. Is there anything that has been the same **generation after generation**? What?

3. When two words come together to form a new word, that new word is called a compound. Some examples of compound words found in the mini-lecture are:

   meat-eating

   fruit-eating

   empty-handed

   Can you think of some others?

## Writing It Down

Taking notes is a quick way to write down information. It is important because it helps us to remember the main ideas in a lecture. Read the following summary of the mini-lecture. Decide which words are the most important. (The sentence has nine important words.) Cross out the words that are not important. Discuss your answers.

*If we would follow a diet similar to that of thousands of years ago, our lives would be better and we would live longer. (9)*

There are many different ways to take notes. Here is one way. One blank means one word. Write the important words in the blanks. USE ABBREVIATIONS AND/OR SYMBOLS IF YOU CAN.

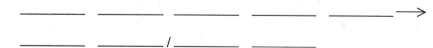

 Listen to the mini-lecture one more time. Look at the notes while listening.

## Following Up

1. Go to the library. Look up the section on "fossils" in the encyclopedia. How does it explain the meaning of *fossil*? Copy a few words from the encyclopedia that explain the word. Make a list of things scientists have learned from studying fossils.

   Definition of *fossil*: _____

   _____

   _____

   _____

   _____

   Scientists have learned the following things from studying fossils:

   a. _____

   b. _____

   c. _____

   d. _____

   e. _____

2. Does the encyclopedia have any pictures of fossils? If so, make photocopies and bring them to class.

3. List the sources for your information:

   Name of encyclopedia _____

   Volume number _____ Year _____ Page(s) _____

4. Read the discussion suggestions, and choose one to talk or write about.
   a. Has your diet changed since coming to the United States? What are some of the changes? Do you think that is good or bad? Why?
   b. Throughout history in different societies men and women did different things. In your country, who was responsible for providing food—men or women? What kind of food? Is that true today?

5. Read the transcripts of both mini-lectures. Highlight the main ideas. Highlight any vocabulary that you do not understand, and find the meanings. Listen to the mini-lectures and follow along with the transcripts.

# SECTION A

## Before You Listen

### Getting Set

Look at the illustrations. How are they the same? How are they different?

### Talking It Over

You will hear a minilecture about vision. Look at the following list of words. Practice saying them. Which words do you think that you will hear? Why? Discuss your answers.

| | | |
|---|---|---|
| age(ing) | focus | near |
| blur(ring) | glasses | old |
| close up | impairment | ophthalmic |
| distance | lens | prescription(s) |
| drugstore | middle-aged | reading |
| eye | muscles | see |
| farsightedness | | |

## Spelling It Out

Read the following definitions of some words from the mini-lecture. Listen to the words that match the definitions. Write down the spelling for each word.

1. _ _ _ _ _ _ _ _ _ : illness or problem

2. _ _ _ _ _ _ _ _ _ : most often

3. _ _ _ _ _ _

   _ _ _    _ _ : don't like

4. _ _ _ _ _ _ _ _ : easily seen

5. _ _ _ _ _ _ _ _ _ _ _ : way to do something

Now practice saying the words.

# As You Listen

 **Checking It Off**

Look at the vocabulary list on page 92. Listen to the mini-lecture. <u>Underline</u> the words that you hear. Discuss your choices.

## Zeroing In: Main Idea

This mini-lecture has one main idea. Read the following sentences. Put an X in front of the most important point. Discuss your choice.

_____ 1. Presbyopia is an eye condition which makes it difficult for the middle-aged to read things easily.

_____ 2. Presbyopia begins at around the age of ten when a person's eyeballs stop growing.

_____ 3. People can choose from reading, bifocal, trifocal, and progressive addition eyeglasses.

_____ 4. Progressive addition lenses do not have lines that divide the lenses into different parts.

 Look at the following phrases. They tell you that main ideas or important points will follow. Listen to the mini-lecture again. <u>Underline</u> the phrase that you hear. Discuss your answers.

1. To summarize, then, . . .

2. What I'd like to talk about today . . .

3. What I have just explained is that . . .

Listen to this phrase from the mini-lecture. Answer the following questions. Discuss your answers.

1. What is the most important word? _____

2. Listen to the mini-lecture again. Does the main idea come at the beginning, the middle, or the end?

# After You Listen

## Practicing New Words

■ The words on the left are from the mini-lecture. Practice saying them. Match the words with their definitions on the right. Discuss your answers.

| | |
|---|---|
| _____ 1. cells | a. ability to move |
| _____ 2. gradually | b. little by little |
| _____ 3. flexibility | c. many different kinds |
| _____ 4. wide range | d. removed |
| _____ 5. announce | e. strength |
| _____ 6. power | f. tell |
| _____ 7. eliminated | g. units of living matter |

■ Practice saying these words from the mini-lecture. Some are adjectives. Some are adverbs.

| *Adjectives* | *Adverbs* |
|---|---|
| 1. good | well |
| 2. eventual | eventually |
| 3. gradual | gradually |
| 4. clear | clearly |
| 5. wide | widely |
| 6. different | differently |
| 7. general | generally |
| 8. total | totally |

■ Read the following sentences. Write the correct form of the word in the blank. Words from number one on the list go in sentence number one, words from number two on the list go in sentence number two, and so forth. Circle whether the word is a noun or a verb.

1. a. How _____ is your vision?   adjective   adverb

   b. I see _____ without wearing glasses.   adjective   adverb

2. a. Almost everyone _____ has to wear glasses.
      adjective     adverb

   b. An _____ result of ageing is having to wear glasses.
      adjective     adverb

3. a. The _____ loss of clear vision begins at age ten.
      adjective     adverb

   b. The lenses _____ lose their flexibility.
      adjective     adverb

4. a. How _____ can you see the chart?   adjective   adverb

   b. On a _____ day you can see forever.
      adjective     adverb

5. a. Contact lenses are _____ used by many people.
      adjective     adverb

   b. That store has a _____ selection of eyeglass frames.
      adjective     adverb

6. a. I think the professor graded the papers _____ this time.
      adjective     adverb

   b. There are many _____ kinds of reading glasses.
      adjective     adverb

7. a. She _____ collects the homework papers before class
      begins.   adjective     adverb

   b. What is your _____ opinion of the class?
      adjective     adverb

8. a. How much was the _____ bill for the eye exam?
      adjective     adverb

   b. The lines on the lenses have been _____ eliminated.
      adjective     adverb

■ Read and discuss the following questions with your classmates.

1. The lecturer said that presbyopia was an eye condition that affects older people. Can you think of some other things that **affect** older people?

2. **Bifocals** are lenses divided into two parts. **Trifocals** are lenses divided into three parts. What other words can you think of which begin with *bi-* and *tri-*? What does each one mean?

3. The lecturer said that the lenses in the eyes gradually lose their flexibility. Can you think of anything else which loses its **flexibility** over a period of time?

## Writing It Down

Taking notes is a quick way to write down information. It is important because it helps us to remember the main ideas in a lecture. Read the summary of the mini-lecture. Decide which words are the most important. (The sentence has five important words.) Cross out the words that are not important. Discuss your answers.

*A fifty-year-old not being able to see very well when doing something like reading has an impairment called presbyopia. (5)*

There are many different ways to take notes. Here is one way. One blank means one word. Write the important words in the blanks. USE ABBREVIATIONS AND/OR SYMBOLS IF YOU CAN.

_____  _____  _____  _____ = _____

Listen to the mini-lecture one more time. Look at the notes while listening.

# SECTION B

## Before You Listen

### Spelling It Out

Read the following definitions of some words from the mini-lecture. Listen to the words that match the definition. Write down the spelling for each word.

1. _ _ _ _ _ _ _ _ : easily frightened people

2. _ _ _ _ _ _

   _ _ _ _ _ : causes

3. _ _ _ _ _ _ _ _ _ _ : specific

4. _ _ _ _ : happens to

5. _ _ _ _ _ : clear

Now practice saying the words.

## As You Listen

 **Checking It Off**

Look at the vocabulary list on page 92. Listen to the mini-lecture. <u>Circle</u> the words that you hear. Discuss your answers with your classmates.

### Zeroing In: Main Idea

This mini-lecture has one main idea. Read the following sentences. Put an X in front of the most important point. Discuss your choice.

_____ 1. As people get older, their vision becomes poorer.

_____ 2. Almost everyone has trouble with his or her vision by the time he or she is fifty years old.

_____ 3. People need new eyeglasses every twelve to eighteen months.

_____ 4. Almost all middle-aged individuals have a form of farsightedness called presbyopia.

Look again at the phrases on page 93 that tell you that main ideas or important points will follow. Listen to the mini-lecture again. <u>Circle</u> the phrase that you hear. Discuss your answer.

     Listen to this phrase from the mini-lecture. Answer the following questions. Discuss your answers.

1. What is the most important word? _____

2. Listen to the mini-lecture again. Does the main idea come at the beginning, the middle, or the end?

## After You Listen

■ The words on the left are from the mini-lecture. Practice saying them. Match the words with their definitions on the right. Discuss your answers.

_____ 1. goes by the name of     a. almost

_____ 2. virtually     b. controlled

_____ 3. research     c. don't have

_____ 4. provided     d. given

_____ 5. clues     e. is called

_____ 6. lack     f. pieces of equipment

_____ 7. regulated     g. studies

_____ 8. devices     h. things which help find answers to questions

■ Some of these words are from the mini-lecture. Look at each group, and circle the word or phrase that does not belong. What are the reasons for your answers?

| | | | |
|---|---|---|---|
| 1. disability | illness | impairment | prescription |
| 2. affects | brings about | happens to | hits |
| 3. almost | always | nearly | virtually |
| 4. investigation | research | studies | suggestion |
| 5. bifocals | contact lenses | progressive addition lenses | trifocals |
| 6. don't have | don't want | lack | need |

■ Read and discuss the following questions with your classmates.

1. **FDA** is the abbreviation for the **Food and Drug Administration,** an agency of the United States government. Do you know any other abbreviations for governmental agencies?

2. The lecturer mentioned the wise saying "Ageing is not for sissies" which means that getting old is difficult, and it takes courage to grow old. Do you know any wise sayings? What does each one mean?

3. You can add *non-* to many English words to make them mean "not." Some examples are:

prescription ⟶ nonprescription

stop            ⟶ nonstop

payment      ⟶ nonpayment

Can you think of some others?

## Writing It Down

Taking notes is a quick way to write down information. It is important because it helps us to remember the main ideas in a lecture. Read the following summary of the mini-lecture. Decide which words are the most important. (The sentence has three important words.) Cross out the words that are not important. Discuss your answers.

*Presbyopia is a form of farsightedness in middle-aged people. (3)*

There are many different ways to take notes. Here is one way. One blank means one word. Write the important words in the blanks. USE ABBREVIATIONS AND/OR SYMBOLS IF YOU CAN.

_____ = _____   _____

 Listen to the mini-lecture one more time. Look at the notes while listening.

## Following Up

1. Go to the library. Look up the section on "eye" or "farsightedness" in the encyclopedia. How does it explain the meaning of *farsightedness*?

Meaning of *farsightedness*: _____

_____

_____

_____

2. Farsightedness is an eye defect. Name two other eye defects listed in the encyclopedia. What does each one mean?

   _____

   _____

   _____

   _____

3. Does the encyclopedia have any pictures or illustrations showing different kinds of eye defects? If so, make photocopies and bring them to class.

4. List the sources for your information:

   Name of encyclopedia _____

   Volume number _____ Year _____ Page(s) _____

5. Read the discussion suggestions, and choose one to talk or write about.
   a. Do you wear glasses or contact lenses? How long have you worn them? How many other family members need vision correction like yourself? How often do you have your eyes checked?
   b. Can you think of other things besides eye problems which afflict forty- or fifty-year-old people? Are there any advantages in getting older? What?

6. Read the transcripts of both mini-lectures. Highlight the main ideas. Highlight any vocabulary that you do not understand, and find the meanings. Listen to the mini-lectures and follow along with the transcripts.

TODAY'S LECTURE

Space
Research

# SECTION A

## Before You Listen

### Getting Set

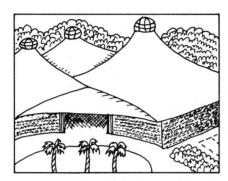 

Look at the illustrations. How do you think the tent is related to the U.S. space program? What do runners and astronauts have in common?

### Talking It Over

You will hear a mini-lecture about space research. Look at the following list of words. Practice saying them. Which words do you think that you will hear? Why? Discuss your answers.

| | | |
|---|---|---|
| applications | expenditures | program |
| benefits | fabric | scienti(-st)(-fic) |
| business | industry | spin-off |
| developed | medicine | suits |
| dried food | money | technology transfers |
| education | NASA | weight |

## Spelling It Out

Read the following definitions of some words from the mini-lecture. Listen to the words that match the definitions. Write down the spelling for each word.

1. __ __ __ __ __ __

    __ __ __ : complete

2. __ __ __ __ __ __ : special words

3. __ __ __ __ __ : area or field of interest

4. __ __ __ __ __ __ : used for the first time

5. __ __ __ __ __ __ : popular

Now practice saying the words.

# As You Listen

 **Checking It Off**

Look at the vocabulary list on page 102. Listen to the mini-lecture. <u>Underline</u> the words that you hear. Discuss your choices.

## Zeroing In: Main Idea

This mini-lecture has one main idea. Read the following sentences. Put an X in front of the most important point. Discuss your choice.

_____ 1. "Spin-off" is NASA jargon for "technology transfer."

_____ 2. Astronauts needed dried food in order to save weight in the space capsule.

_____ 3. The field which has benefited the most from space research is medicine.

_____ 4. The space program more than pays for itself in the many benefits it provides the world.

 Look at the following phrases. They tell you that main ideas or important points will follow. Listen to the mini-lecture again. <u>Underline</u> the phrase that you hear. Discuss your answers.

1. One could conclude . . .
2. Simply stated, . . .
3. Today, we are going to discuss . . .

Listen to this phrase from the mini-lecture. Answer the following questions. Discuss your answers.

1. What is the most important word? _____

2. Listen to the mini-lecture again. Does the main idea come at the beginning, the middle, or the end?

# After You Listen

## Practicing New Words

■ The words on the left are from the mini-lecture. Practice saying them. Match the words with their definitions on the right. Discuss your answers.

| | |
|---|---|
| _____ 1. term | a. actually |
| _____ 2. are familiar with | b. as completely different from |
| _____ 3. series | c. caused by |
| _____ 4. as opposed to | d. continuing program |
| _____ 5. literally | e. discovered |
| _____ 6. occurred | f. don't know |
| _____ 7. aren't aware of | g. happened |
| _____ 8. came across | h. know about |
| _____ 9. marathon joggers | i. long-distance runners |
| _____ 10. attributed to | j. word |

■ Practice saying these words from the mini-lecture. Some are nouns and some are verbs.

| *Nouns* | *Verbs* |
|---|---|
| 1. discussion | discuss |
| 2. flight | fly |
| 3. invention | invent |
| 4. beneficiary | benefit |
| 5. occurrence | occur |
| 6. weight | weigh |
| 7. complaint | complain |
| 8. development | develop |
| 9. communication | communicate |
| 10. conclusion | conclude |

■ Read the following sentences. Write the correct form of the word in the blank. Words from number one on the list go in sentence number one, words from number two on the list go in sentence number two, and so forth. Circle whether the word is a noun or a verb.

1. a. Let's _____ all the advantages of space research.

   noun     verb

   b. Our _____ about space research was not finished

   yesterday.   noun     verb

2. a. If you were an astronaut, would you want to _____ to

   the moon?   noun     verb

   b. Tomorrow the lecture will be on the physics of space

   _____.   noun     verb

3. a. Hurry up and _____ a reason for not going to class.

   noun     verb

   b. The word *spin-off* is an _____ of a NASA scientist.

   noun     verb

4. a. Who will be the _____ of all these medical advances?

   noun     verb

   b. You will greatly _____ from all the space research that

   has been done.   noun     verb

5. a. Did it _____ to you that taking good notes in class is

   important?   noun     verb

   b. What single _____ in the history of space travel do you

   remember best?   noun     verb

6. a. How much does the space capsule _____ ?

   noun     verb

   b. The _____ of the space capsule was not known.

   noun     verb

7. a. Their space suits were so hot that the astronauts made a

   _____.   noun     verb

   b. Why did the astronauts _____ about the clothing?

   noun     verb

8. a. People have benefited from the _____ of a light-weight

   wheelchair.  noun    verb

   b. Space research made it possible to _____ many medical

   devices.  noun    verb

9. a. I think the instructor's _____ with the students needs to

   be improved.  noun    verb

   b. Paramedics can _____ with hospitals with this device.

   noun    verb

10. a. The _____ of her lecture is also found on page 200 in

   the textbook.  noun    verb

   b. What can you _____ from the lecture?  noun    verb

■ Read and discuss the following questions with your classmates.

1. The lecturer used the word **capsule,** meaning "compartment" or
   "space where astronauts live." It also can mean "a small amount of
   medicine, something like a pill." Look at the following words from the
   lecture. Think of as many different meanings as you can.
   • folks
   • term
   • light

2. You can add -*less* to many English words to make them adjectives.
   Some examples are:

   count ⎯⎯⎯→ countless (cannot be counted)

   hope ⎯⎯⎯→ hopeless (without hope)

   tire ⎯⎯⎯→ tireless (never getting tired)

   Can you think of some others? What are their meanings?

3. Words ending in -*ics* are nouns. Some examples from the lecture are:

   **diabetics** (people who have diabetes)

   **paramedics** (people who help take care of the sick)

   How many others can you list? What are their meanings?

### Writing It Down

Taking notes is a quick way to write down information. It is important because it helps us to remember the main ideas in a lecture. Read the summary of the mini-lecture. Decide which words are the most important. (The sentence has six important words.) Cross out the words that are not important. Discuss your answers.

*The U.S. space program produces many more benefits to the world than what it costs. (6)*

There are many different ways to take notes. Here is one way. One blank means one word. Write the important words in the blanks. USE ABBREVIATIONS AND/OR SYMBOLS IF YOU CAN.

_____  _____ : _____  _____  _____  _____

 Listen to the mini-lecture one more time. Look at the notes while listening.

# SECTION B

# Before You Listen

### Spelling It Out

Read the following definitions of some words from the mini-lecture. Listen to the words that match the definition. Write down the spelling for each word.

1. _ _ _ _ _ _ _ : deserved

2. _ _ _ _ _ _ _ : exact

3. _ _ _ _ _ _ _ _ : large

4. _ _ _ _ _ _ _ : quality

5. _ _ _ _ _ _ _ _ : think about

Now practice saying the words.

# As You Listen

 **Checking It Off**

Look at the vocabulary list on page 102. Listen to the mini-lecture. Circle the words that you hear. Discuss your answers with your class-mates.

## Zeroing In: Main Idea

This mini-lecture has one main idea. Read the following sentences. Put an X in front of the most important point. Discuss your choice.

_____ 1. The U.S. space program has produced spin-offs called "technology transfers."

_____ 2. The U.S. space program has a huge cost, but the world benefits even more.

_____ 3. The actual value of NASA's transfer technology is not possible to figure because there is so much transfer.

_____ 4. Elderly people have been helped because of NASA's development of externally worn programmable devices.

Look again at the phrases on page 103 that tell you that main ideas or important points will follow. Listen to the mini-lecture again. Circle the phrase that you hear. Discuss your answer.

Listen to this phrase from the mini-lecture. Answer the following questions. Discuss your answers.

1. What is the most important word? _____

2. Listen to the mini-lecture again. Does the main idea come at the beginning, the middle, or the end?

# After You Listen

## Practicing New Words

■ The words on the left are from the mini-lecture. Practice saying them. Match the words with their definitions on the right. Discuss your answers.

| | | | |
|---|---|---|---|
| _____ 1. based on | | a. | depending on which one is true |
| _____ 2. character | | b. | good of everyone |
| _____ 3. as the case may be | | c. | greatness of size |
| _____ 4. practices | | d. | help |
| _____ 5. products | | e. | not important |
| _____ 6. public welfare | | f. | person in a play |
| _____ 7. pilgrims | | g. | religious travelers |
| _____ 8. frivolous | | h. | things which are done |
| _____ 9. magnitude | | i. | things which are made |
| _____ 10. boon | | j. | used as a starting point |

■ Some of these words are from the mini-lecture. Look at each group, and circle the word or phrase that does not belong. What are the reasons for your answers?

| | | | |
|---|---|---|---|
| 1. concerns | is about | leads to | refers to |
| 2. practical | theoretical | useful | workable |
| 3. formerly | in the beginning | originally | specifically |
| 4. Chicago | Jerusalem | Mecca | Rome |
| 5. commercial districts | residential areas | shopping centers | shopping malls |
| 6. cutting back | cutting off | decreasing | reducing |
| 7. first | most important | primary | secondary |
| 8. benefit | concern | interest | worry |
| 9. estimate | guess | know | predict |
| 10. conceivably | imaginably | possibly | terribly |
| 11. consider | include | take into account | take out of |
| 12. generated | made | produced | transferred |
| 13. alloys | brass | copper | steel |
| 14. bound to | kept to | refer to | tied to |
| 15. placed | stored | stowed | used |
| 16. hindered | made difficult for | not helped | sacrificed |

■ Read and discuss the following questions with your classmates.

1. *Self* is used at the beginning of words to mean "of or by oneself." Some examples from the mini-lecture are:

   **self-esteem** (your opinion about yourself)

   **self-medication** (giving yourself medicine)

   Can you think of some others? What do they mean?

2. The lecturer said that lighter-weight wheelchairs have given handicapped people **access** to air travel, meaning that travel by air is easier now. What other things have given the handicapped greater access to life in general?

3. The lecturer mentioned a **weather satellite** that follows storms, making it possible to warn people about bad weather. What other satellites do you know about? What do they do?

## Writing It Down

Taking notes is a quick way to write down information. It is important because it helps us to remember the main ideas in a lecture. Read the following summary of the mini-lecture. Decide which words are the most important. (The sentence has six important words.) Cross out the words that are not important. Discuss your answers.

*Benefits to the world far exceed the cost of the U.S. space program. (6)*

There are many different ways to take notes. Here is one way. One blank means one word. Write the important words in the blanks. USE ABBREVIATIONS AND/OR SYMBOLS IF YOU CAN.

_____  _____  _____  _____  _____  _____

 Listen to the mini-lecture one more time. Look at the notes while listening.

**Following Up**

1. Go to the library. Look up "space" in the encyclopedia. How is the term *satellite* defined? How many kinds of satellites are listed? What are their functions?

   Definition of *satellite*: _____

   _____

   _____

   *Kinds of satellites*                    *Uses*

   a.

   b.

   c.

   d.

   e.

2. If there are any illustrations showing satellites, make a photocopy and bring it to class.

3. List the sources of your information:

   Name of encyclopedia _____

   Volume number _____  Year _____  Page(s) _____

4. Read the discussion suggestions, and choose one to talk or write about.
   a. Many people feel that money spent on space research could be better used here on earth. How do you feel about this? Why?
   b. Have you ever done any research? When? Why did you do it? What were the results?

5. Read the transcripts of both mini-lectures. Highlight the main ideas. Highlight any vocabulary that you do not understand, and find the meanings. Listen to the mini-lectures and follow along with the transcripts.

# PART TWO

TODAY'S LECTURE

Termites

# Before You Listen

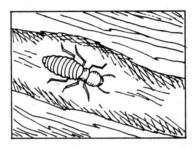

Termites are said to be like ants and bees.

Can you think of any similarities?

**Talking It Over**

You will hear a mini-lecture about termites. Look at the following list of words. Practice saying them. Which words do you think that you will hear? Why? Discuss your answers.

| | |
|---|---|
| amphibian | pests |
| burrow | queen |
| chicken | social insect |
| colonies | soldiers |
| damage | swarm |
| guns | wings |
| king | wood |
| nests | workers |

## As You Listen

 **Checking It Off**

Look at the vocabulary list. Listen to the mini-lecture. Circle the words that you hear. Discuss your choices.

### Zeroing In: Main Idea

This mini-lecture has one main idea. Read the following sentences. Put an X in front of the most important point. Discuss your choice.

_____ 1. The termite causes millions of dollars of damage each year.

_____ 2. The termite lives underground with millions of other termites.

_____ 3. There are three different kinds of termites in a colony.

_____ 4. It is difficult to see termites.

### Zeroing In: Supporting Details

Read the following details from the mini-lecture. Put an X in front of the *three* details which support the main idea.

_____ 1. Termites are called "white ants" in some parts of the country.

_____ 2. Termites are related to cockroaches.

_____ 3. Termites swarm in order to build new nests.

_____ 4. The queen produces new members by laying up to 50,000 eggs a year.

_____ 5. The soldiers or guards protect the colony.

_____ 6. The workers burrow and eat the wood.

## After You Listen

### In Other Words

The following sentences are from the mini-lecture. Look at the under-lined words. Practice saying them. Then choose their meanings.

1. The guards can <u>withstand</u> some exposure to light.
   a. enjoy
   b. hide from
   c. look for
   d. take

2. These termites are very <u>sensitive</u> to light.

   a. afraid to show the effect of
   b. happy to show the effect of
   c. quick to show the effect of
   d. slow to show the effect of

3. We <u>rarely</u> see termites.

   a. not often          c. sometimes
   b. often              d. usually

4. You are <u>enveloped in</u> a cloud of insects.

   a. chosen by          c. surrounded by
   b. sent into          d. taken into

5. This dangerous pest is very difficult to <u>detect</u> until it is too late.

   a. examine            c. kill
   b. find               d. stop

## Writing It Down

Read the following two summaries of the mini-lecture. Choose the *one* summary that best represents the lecture. Then decide which words are the most important, and arrange them in the note-taking form you want. Discuss your answers.

*Summary #1*

One can see three different kinds of termites in a colony. The first is a queen who produces new members, the second is a guard who protects the colony, and the third is a worker.

*Summary #2*

Termites cause millions of dollars in property damage each year, and they are not easy to see. They live in underground colonies and do not like the light.

I chose Summary #_____ .

My notes: _____

_____

_____

_____

_____

Listen to the mini-lecture one more time. Look at the notes while
listening.

## Following Up

1. Go to the library. Look up the sections on "termites," "bees," and
   "ants" in the encyclopedia. Make a list of things the three have in
   common.
2. List the source for your information:

   Name of encyclopedia _____

   Volume number _____  Year _____  Page(s) _____
3. Read the discussion suggestions, and choose one to talk or write about.
   a. Of all the insects in the world, which ones do you dislike the most?
      Why? Are there any which you like? Why?
   b. How many kinds of creatures can you think of that build nests?
      Are sensitive to light? Lay eggs?
4. Read the transcripts of the mini-lecture. Highlight the main idea.
   Highlight any vocabulary that you do not understand, and find the
   meanings. Listen to the mini-lecture and follow along with the
   transcript.

# UNIT TWELVE

### TODAY'S LECTURE

# Communication Styles

# Before You Listen

## Getting Set

Does a man speak to a woman in the same way that a man speaks to a man? That a woman speaks to a woman?

What are some differences?

## Talking It Over

You will hear a minilecture about communication styles. Look at the following list of words. Practice saying them. Which words do you think that you will hear? Why? Discuss your answers.

circus                          misinterpret
clothing                        nonverbal
fashion                         plastic
gender                          sexes
intonation                      solar
language                        tone

# As You Listen

 **Checking It Off**

Look at the vocabulary list. Listen to the mini-lecture. Circle the words that you hear. Discuss your choices.

## Zeroing In: Main Idea

This mini-lecture has one main idea. Read the following sentences. Put an X in front of the most important point. Discuss your choice.

_____ 1. Men and women communicate differently.

_____ 2. A woman is more likely to use rising intonation when answering the phone.

_____ 3. Nonverbal communication means gestures, facial expressions, and tone of voice.

_____ 4. Trouble between men and women comes from the differences in the way they communicate.

## Zeroing In: Supporting Details

Read the following details from the mini-lecture. Put an X in front of the *two* details which support the main idea.

_____ 1. Differences in the way men and women communicate can be found at all levels.

_____ 2. Men and women are different.

_____ 3. Nonverbal communication is understood differently by men and women.

_____ 4. There are differences in intonation between men and women.

# After You Listen

## In Other Words

The following sentences are from the mini-lecture. Look at the underlined words. Practice saying them. Then, choose their meanings.

1. A woman, when she answers the telephone, is more <u>apt</u> to say "Hello" with rising intonation.

    a. eager             c. likely

    b. happy           d. pleased

2. Nonverbal communication here means <u>gestures</u>.

   a. arm movements            c. eye movements
   b. body movements          d. head movements

3. The man maybe <u>ignores</u> the sarcastic tone or the fact that the woman has turned away.

   a. listens to and forgets      c. pays no attention to
   b. listens to and remembers   d. pays some attention to

4. The woman has turned away from him when <u>denying</u> that she is angry.

   a. saying maybe            c. saying probably
   b. saying no               d. saying yes

5. Troubles between men and women can be <u>attributed</u> to the differences in communication styles.

   a. caused by               c. observed in
   b. noticed in               d. settled by

## Writing It Down

Read the following two summaries of the mini-lecture. Choose the *one* summary that best represents the lecture. Then, decide which words are the most important, and arrange them in the note-taking form you want. Discuss your answers.

*Summary #1*

Men and women use different intonations when communicating. This is proven by the fact that women often use rising intonation when answering the phone, while men use falling or level intonation.

*Summary #2*

The sexes do not communicate with each other in the same way. This is proven by the fact that men and women have differences in their intonation and do not understand nonverbal communication in the same way.

I chose Summary #_____ .

My notes: _____

_____

_____

_____

_____

Listen to the mini-lecture one more time. Look at the notes while listening.

## Following Up

1. Consult your campus telephone directory for the numbers of various important offices (health center, library, dean of students, admissions and records, etc.). Call the office and listen for the following:
   - words spoken to answer the phone
   - intonation used (rising, falling, level)
   - sex of person answering the phone

   Report your findings back to the class.

2. Read the discussion suggestions, and choose one to talk or write about.
   a. In addition to communication styles, can you think of other areas where women and men are different? Give examples from your own experience.
   b. What kinds of information can be communicated with only gestures and facial expressions (nonverbal communication)? Are these gestures and facial expressions the same all over the world?

3. Read the transcript of the mini-lecture. Highlight the main idea. Highlight any vocabulary that you do not understand, and find the meanings. Listen to the mini-lecture and follow along with the transcript.

TODAY'S LECTURE

Domesticating
Wild Animals

# Before You Listen

## Getting Set

Today, why are some animals tame and others wild?
Has this situation always been true?

## Talking It Over

You will hear a mini-lecture about domesticating wild animals. Look at the following list of words. Practice saying them. Which words do you think that you will hear? Why? Discuss your answers.

| | |
|---|---|
| aggressors | rearing |
| ancient | salad |
| automobiles | tame |
| breeding | trained |
| computers | trapped |
| hunted | victims |
| pets | vitamins |

# As You Listen

 **Checking It Off**

Look at the vocabulary list. Listen to the mini-lecture. Circle the words that you hear. Discuss your choices.

## Zeroing In: Main Idea

This mini-lecture has one main idea. Read the following sentences. Put an X in front of the most important point. Discuss your choice.

_____ 1. People domesticated wild animals.

_____ 2. Animals in nature are only as wild as they need to be in order to survive.

_____ 3. Dogs are domesticated wolves.

_____ 4. People had to domesticate themselves before animals were domesticated.

## Zeroing In: Supporting Details

Read the following details from the mini-lecture. Put an X in front of the *two* details which support the main idea.

_____ 1. Animals usually run away instead of fighting.

_____ 2. Animals will continue to play an important part in people's lives.

_____ 3. At first, ancient people looked at animals as sources of food and tools.

_____ 4. Domestication probably occurred through the keeping and raising of young animals.

_____ 5. Self-taming occurs when animals begin staying around places where people are.

# After You Listen

## In Other Words

The following sentences are from the mini-lecture. Look at the underlined words. Practice saying them. Then, choose their meanings.

1. People often say that people <u>domesticated</u> wild animals.

    a. ate
    b. killed
    c. scared
    d. tamed

2. People were usually the <u>aggressors</u>.

    a. farmers
    b. hunters
    c. leaders
    d. survivors

3. Domestication probably occurred through the keeping and <u>rearing</u> of young animals.

    a. feeding
    b. raising
    c. selling
    d. watering

4. One key factor in the <u>origins</u> of domestication had to be the changes in human attitudes and behavior.

    a. amount
    b. beginnings
    c. endings
    d. process

5. Ancient people <u>regarded</u> animals simply as food.

    a. bought
    b. sold
    c. thought of
    d. wrote about

## Writing It Down

Read the following two summaries of the mini-lecture. Choose the *one* summary that best represents the lecture. Then, decide which words are the most important, and arrange them in the note-taking form you want. Discuss your answers.

*Summary #1*

Animals were domesticated only after ancient peoples domesticated themselves. In the beginning, people used animals only as a source of food and tools. This changed when people began keeping and raising young animals.

*Summary #2*

As far as domestication is concerned, birds and animals can be ranked into three groups. The first group is animals that are not wild as adults, such as dolphins and seals. The second is animals that are tamed while young and have their breeding controlled, like dogs and horses. The third is animals that can be tamed, such as elephants.

I chose Summary #_____ .

My notes: _____

_____

_____

_____

_____

_____

_____

_____

_____

_____

 Listen to the mini-lecture one more time. Look at the notes while listening.

## Following Up

1. The pet industry is big business in the United States today. Go out of the classroom and interview ten people (not your classmates). Find out the following:
   - Do they have a pet at home?
   - If so, what kind of pet is it?
   - How much money do they spend on their pet each year?

   Summarize your results, and report your findings back to the class.

2. Read the discussion suggestions, and choose one to talk or write about.
   a. Are there advantages in having a pet? What are they? How about disadvantages?
   b. Many times, people from different cultures and countries treat animals differently. Do people in your country feel the same way as Americans do about animals? What are the differences?

3. Read the transcript of the mini-lecture. Highlight the main idea. Highlight any vocabulary that you do not understand, and find the meanings. Listen to the mini-lecture and follow along with the transcript.

TODAY'S LECTURE

Bread and Beer

# Before You Listen

## Getting Set

What connection can you think of between bread and beer?

Which do you think came first?

## Talking It Over

You will hear a mini-lecture about bread and beer. Look at the follow-ing list of words. Practice saying them. Which words do you think that you will hear? Why? Discuss your answers.

| | |
|---|---|
| agricultural | foodstuffs |
| alcoholic beverage | ground down |
| bakery | milk |
| brewery | tobacco |
| cereals | wild grains |
| chewing gum | wild grasses |

# As You Listen

 Checking It Off

Look at the vocabulary list. Listen to the mini-lecture. Circle the words that you hear. Discuss your choices.

### Zeroing In: Main Idea

This mini-lecture has one main idea. Read the following sentences. Put an X in front of the most important point. Discuss your choice.

_____ 1. The domestication of wild grains was important in the change of our civilization from a hunter-gatherer society to an agricultural one.

_____ 2. Early man discovered by accident that wild grasses could be used for making bread.

_____ 3. Through another accident, it was discovered that wild grasses could also be used for making beer.

_____ 4. Recent discoveries in the Tigris and Euphrates valleys suggest that man discovered how to make beer first.

### Zeroing In: Supporting Details

Read the following details from the mini-lecture. Put an X in front of the *one* detail that supports the main idea.

_____ 1. Beer became an important part of religious customs.

_____ 2. Early man discovered by accident that wild grasses could be used for making beer and bread.

_____ 3. It was first thought that early man discovered how to make bread and then beer.

_____ 4. Wild grasses mixed with water and other plants produced beer.

## After You Listen

### In Other Words

The following sentences are from the mini-lecture. Look at the underlined words. Practice saying them. Then choose their meanings.

1. The <u>domestication</u> of wild grains was a milestone.
   a. buying
   b. farming
   c. selling
   d. understanding

2. It was the transition of our civilization from a <u>mobile</u> hunter society to a more agricultural one.
   - a. large
   - b. moving
   - c. quiet
   - d. successful

3. They discovered through some <u>fortuitous</u> accident that certain wild grasses could be made into food.
   - a. easy
   - b. lucky
   - c. terrible
   - d. unlucky

4. Wild grasses could be ground down and made into a <u>portable</u> food supply.
   - a. easy to eat
   - b. easy to make
   - c. easy to move
   - d. easy to sell

5. Beer became an <u>integral</u> part of their society.
   - a. important
   - b. small
   - c. useful
   - d. wonderful

## Writing It Down

Read the following two summaries of the mini-lecture. Choose the *one* summary that best represents the lecture. Then, decide which words are the most important, and arrange them in the note-taking form you want. Discuss your answers.

*Summary #1*

Early man discovered that beer could be made from wild grasses. After beer became an important part of the society, the way to make cereal and bread from these wild grasses was discovered.

*Summary #2*

When man learned how to grow wild grain, civilization changed from a society of hunters to an agricultural one. The change occurred by accident when man learned that beer, bread, and cereal could be made from wild grasses.

I chose Summary #_____ .

My notes: _____

_____

_____

_____

_____

Listen to the mini-lecture one more time. Look at the notes while listening.

## Following Up

1. Find out where the Tigris and Euphrates valleys are. Consult references and discover why this part of the world is considered so important in history.
   Report your findings back to the class.

2. Read the discussion suggestions and choose one to talk or write about.
   a. What ingredients are needed for making bread? For making beer? Have you ever made either?
   b. Throughout history, many different things have been discovered by accident. Can you think of some?

3. Read the transcript of the mini-lecture. Highlight the main idea. Highlight any vocabulary that you do not understand, and find the meanings. Listen to the mini-lecture and follow along with the transcript.

TODAY'S LECTURE

# The New Dark Ages

# Before You Listen

## Getting Set

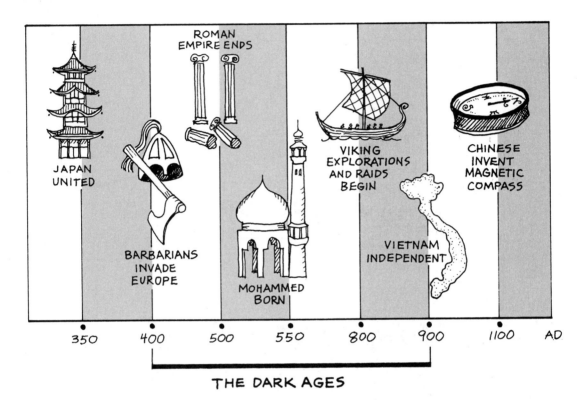

THE DARK AGES

Do you know anything about the Dark Ages, a period in history hundreds of years ago?

Why was that time called "dark"?

## Talking It Over

You will hear a mini-lecture about the new Dark Ages. Look at the following list of words. Practice saying them. Which words do you think that you will hear? Why? Discuss your answers.

| | | |
|---|---|---|
| athletics | enrollment | tuition |
| candle | faculty | uneducated |
| college | learned | university |
| cultured | piano | war |
| degree | students | |

# As You Listen

### Checking It Off

Look at the vocabulary list. Listen to the mini-lecture. Circle the words that you hear. Discuss your choices.

### Zeroing In: Main Idea

This mini-lecture has one main idea. Read the following sentences. Put an X in front of the most important point. Discuss your choice.

_____ 1. Only the rich will be able to go to college in the future.

_____ 2. Aid to education has been decreased.

_____ 3. There has been an increase in research sponsored by private industry.

_____ 4. More and more universities will be closing their doors in the future.

### Zeroing In: Supporting Details

Read the following details from the mini-lecture. Put an X in front of the *two* details which support the main idea.

_____ 1. By the year 2000, birth rates will be too low to maintain the system we have today.

_____ 2. IBM has a program which offers free tuition.

_____ 3. The poor and working class will be unable to attend college because of tuition expenses.

_____ 4. The public has become unhappy with higher education.

_____ 5. Tuition costs have risen 9% in the last four years.

# After You Listen

### In Other Words

The following sentences are from the mini-lecture. Look at the under-lined words. Practice saying them. Then, choose their meanings.

1. Are we looking at the demise of the American college and university system as we know it today?
   a. birth               c. mistakes
   b. death               d. successes

2. The baby boom generation is not reproducing like their parents did.
   a. people born in the late forties and fifties
   b. people born in the sixties and seventies
   c. people born on the East Coast
   d. people born on the West Coast

3. There won't be enough births to sustain the college and university system.
   a. keep at a different level
   b. keep at the same level
   c. move to a higher level
   d. move to a lower level

4. There has been a public disenchantment with higher education.
   a. entertainment
   b. happiness
   c. opposition
   d. unhappiness

5. Colleges are going coed.
   a. both intelligent and not so intelligent
   b. both men and women
   c. both rich and poor
   d. both young and old

## Writing It Down

Read the following two summaries of the mini-lecture. Choose the *one* summary that best represents the lecture. Then, decide which words are the most important, and arrange them in the note-taking form you want. Discuss your answers.

*Summary #1*

Colleges have had to do various things in order to increase their enrollments. Not only have standards been lowered, but colleges now look for older, nontraditional students. They also are merging with other schools and going coeducational.

*Summary #2*

Many colleges and universities will be forced to stop operating in the future. One of the reasons is that college is becoming too expensive for both the poor and middle classes. Another reason is that birth rates by 2000 will not be high enough to sustain today's system.

I chose Summary #_____ .

My notes: _____

_____

_____

_____

Listen to the mini-lecture one more time. Look at the notes while listening.

## Following Up

1. Ask the Admissions and Records Office how many students attend your school at the present time. Compare that number to figures for the last five years. Find out what your school has done to increase its enrollment. Report your findings back to the class.

2. Read the discussion suggestions and choose one to talk or write about.
   a. Do you think that everyone should go to college? Why or why not?
   b. How much does your education cost each semester? Tuition? Books and supplies? Other expenses? Who is paying the bills?

3. Read the transcript of the mini-lecture. Highlight the main idea. Highlight any vocabulary that you do not understand, and find the meanings. Listen to the mini-lecture and follow along with the transcript.

# Before You Listen

## Getting Set

How many different ways are there for keeping food from spoiling for a long time?

What are the advantages and disadvantages of each method?

## Talking It Over

You will hear a minilecture about irradiated food. Look at the following list of words. Practice saying them. Which words do you think that you will hear? Why? Discuss your answers.

| | | | |
|---|---|---|---|
| bacteria | destroy | nuclear | technology |
| cement | hunger | produce | television |
| chemical | library | professor | toxic |
| contaminate | meats | radioactive | trees |

# As You Listen

 **Checking It Off**

Look at the vocabulary list. Listen to the mini-lecture. Circle the words that you hear. Discuss your choices.

## Zeroing In: Main Idea

This mini-lecture has one main idea. Read the following sentences. Put an X in front of the most important point. Discuss your choice.

_____ 1. Some think world hunger can be ended with the use of irradiated food.

_____ 2. Large amounts of gamma radiation are used to irradiate food.

_____ 3. Irradiation produces new substances called "unique radiolytic products."

_____ 4. Other countries will certainly follow the United States in using the irradiation process.

## Zeroing In: Supporting Details

Read the following details from the mini-lecture. Put an X in front of the *two* details which support the main idea.

_____ 1. In the not-so-distant future, the irradiation process will be used more everywhere.

_____ 2. Irradiation causes some chemical changes in food.

_____ 3. Irradiation destroys bacteria and insects that harm the things we eat.

_____ 4. Some people say irradiated food is dangerous.

_____ 5. There has not been enough experimentation done to find out what the effects of irradiation are.

# After You Listen

## In Other Words

The following sentences are from the mini-lecture. Look at the underlined words. Practice saying them. Then, choose their meanings.

1. Its opponents say that irradiated food is a dangerous <u>fraud</u>.
   a. gift
   b. product
   c. something true
   d. something false

2. Irradiation is <u>on the verge of</u> a very dramatic expansion.
   a. at the beginning of
   b. at the end of
   c. in the middle of
   d. in the process of

3. Irradiation is the subjecting of food to <u>massive</u> doses of gamma radiation.
   a. bad
   b. good
   c. large
   d. small

4. There should be a study of the possible <u>toxic</u> effects of "unique radiolytic products."
   a. healthful
   b. long-term
   c. poisonous
   d. side

5. Irradiation does destroy or <u>deplete</u> essential nutrients.
   a. complete
   b. decrease
   c. increase
   d. strengthen

## Writing It Down

Read the following two summaries of the mini-lecture. Choose the *one* summary that best represents the lecture. Then, decide which words are the most important, and arrange them in the note-taking form you want. Discuss your answers.

*Summary #1*

Irradiation causes food to lose some important vitamins. Some say other ways of processing food do the same thing, while others think the body needs those vitamins to deal with the chemicals that irradiated food contains.

*Summary #2*

Irradiation is the subjecting of food to gamma radiation in order to kill bacteria and insects that destroy or spoil meats and produce. Although the process does not make food radioactive, it causes some chemical changes.

I chose Summary #_____ .

My notes: _____

_____

_____

_____

_____

 Listen to the mini-lecture one more time. Look at the notes while listening.

**Following Up**

1. Go to the library and find out all you can about the Food and Drug Administration (FDA). What does it do? How does it do it? Report back to the class.

2. Read the article on irradiated food found in *The Ecologist* (vol. 1b, no. 6, 1986, pp. 270–272).

3. Read the discussion suggestions, and choose one to talk or write about.
   a. Millions of people in the world do not have enough food to eat. Why? What can be done to solve this problem?
   b. The nuclear industry produces radioactive waste. What other kinds of waste materials can you think of? What can be done with them?

4. Read the transcript of the mini-lecture. Highlight the main idea. Highlight any vocabulary that you do not understand, and find the meanings. Listen to the mini-lecture and follow along with the transcript.

TODAY'S LECTURE

The Torpedo Ray

# Before You Listen

How do you suppose the torpedo ray gets its food?

Does its name help you make a guess?

### Talking It Over

You will hear a mini-lecture about torpedo rays. Look at the following list of words. Practice saying them. Which words do you think that you will hear? Why? Discuss your answers.

| | |
|---|---|
| electric shock | sea level |
| engine | stuns |
| fish | swims |
| generate | tail |
| horse | tidal zone |
| mountain | time zone |
| oceans | volts |

# As You Listen

 **Checking It Off**

Look at the vocabulary list. Listen to the mini-lecture. Circle the words that you hear. Discuss your choices.

### Zeroing In: Main Idea

This mini-lecture has one main idea. Read the following sentences. Put an X in front of the most important point. Discuss your choice.

_____ 1. The torpedo ray has a thick tail attached to its round, flat body.

_____ 2. Torpedo rays can be found in oceans all over the world.

_____ 3. Torpedo rays are special because they can produce electricity.

_____ 4. The ancient Greeks used torpedo rays to treat illnesses and diseases.

### Zeroing In: Supporting Details

Read the following details from the mini-lecture. Put an X in front of the *two* details which support the main idea.

_____ 1. Its ability to produce an electric shock helps the torpedo ray to frighten its enemies.

_____ 2. People with certain illnesses were asked to touch the torpedo ray.

_____ 3. Torpedo rays can generate up to 50 volts of electricity.

_____ 4. Torpedo rays can weigh up to sixty pounds.

_____ 5. Torpedo rays get food by stunning fish with an electric shock.

# After You Listen

### In Other Words

The following sentences are from the mini-lecture. Look at the underlined words. Practice saying them. Then choose their meanings.

1. The torpedo ray's size varies.
   a. is different
   b. is large
   c. is small
   d. is the same

2. What is interesting about the torpedo ray is its <u>unique</u> ability to generate electricity.

   a. common             c. strong
   b. special            d. weak

3. The torpedo ray <u>enfolds</u> the fish in its wings.

   a. bends              c. pushes
   b. breaks up          d. wraps up

4. The torpedo ray has a practical purpose found by the <u>ancient</u> Greeks.

   a. very boring        c. very old
   b. very intelligent   d. very young

5. If they were <u>cured</u>, they were asked to touch the ray again.

   a. admired            c. helped
   b. harmed             d. protected

## Writing It Down

Read the following two summaries of the mini-lecture. Choose the *one* summary that best represents the lecture. Then, decide which words are the most important, and arrange them in the note-taking form you want. Discuss your answers.

*Summary #1*

The torpedo ray is unique because it has the special ability to generate electricity. This ability is used for getting food and scaring away its enemies.

*Summary #2*

Torpedo rays weigh up to sixty pounds and can be found in all the temperate and tropical oceans of the world. They live at all depths in the ocean down to 3,000 feet below sea level.

I chose Summary #_____ .

My notes: _____

_____

_____

_____

_____

 Listen to the mini-lecture one more time. Look at the notes while listening.

**Following Up**

1. Go to the library and read the article on torpedo rays found in *Skin Diver* (June 1987, pp. 152–154).

2. Read the discussion suggestions, and choose one to talk or write about.
   a. Which animals living in the ocean do you either like or dislike? Why?
   b. Different animals scare away their enemies in different ways. How many can you think of? Have you ever seen this happen?

3. Read the transcript of the mini-lecture. Highlight the main idea. Highlight any vocabulary that you do not understand, and find the meanings. Listen to the mini-lecture and follow along with the transcript.

TODAY'S LECTURE

Transplants

# Before You Listen

### Getting Set

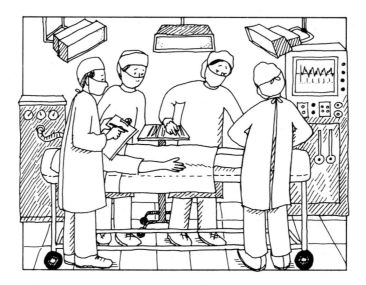

How many different body organs can you think of that have been transplanted successfully?

What are some of the problems in transplanting organs?

### Talking It Over

You will hear a minilecture about transplants. Look at the following list of words. Practice saying them. Which words do you think that you will hear? Why? Discuss your answers.

| | |
|---|---|
| beach | heart |
| body parts | kidneys |
| brain cells | muscles |
| dictionary | operation |
| diseases | organ |
| drug | replacements |
| flower | school |

# As You Listen

**Checking It Off**

> Look at the vocabulary list. Listen to the mini-lecture. Circle the words that you hear. Discuss your choices.

## Zeroing In: Main Idea

> This mini-lecture has one main idea. Read the following sentences. Put an X in front of the most important point. Discuss your choice.

_____ 1. Certain kinds of organ transplants have become very common.

_____ 2. Cyclosporine is a drug which helps the body to accept the transplant.

_____ 3. A normal child might be changed into a genius by transplanting the right type of cells.

_____ 4. With the use of transplants, people's lives will be much improved in the future.

## Zeroing In: Supporting Details

> Read the following details from the mini-lecture. Put an X in front of the _two_ details which support the main idea.

_____ 1. A person's mental ability, strength, or beauty all might be improved by transplants.

_____ 2. Diseased or worn out body parts will be removed and replaced by a transplant.

_____ 3. Muscles from an athlete killed in a car crash might increase the strength of another person.

_____ 4. Scientists have succeeded in making a heart for a dog out of muscles taken from that dog's back.

_____ 5. Thousands of kidneys are transplanted every year.

# After You Listen

## In Other Words

The following sentences are from the mini-lecture. Look at the underlined words. Practice saying them. Then, choose their meanings.

1. These days, certain types of organ transplants have become absolutely <u>routine</u>.

   a. common
   b. difficult
   c. easy
   d. special

2. This drug helps prevent the body's rejection of <u>foreign tissue</u>.

   a. the diseased organ
   b. the normal organ
   c. the transplanted organ
   d. the worn organ

3. Introducing new brain cells into the brains of older people might allow them to recover some of their mental <u>vigor</u>.

   a. conditions
   b. problems
   c. honesty
   d. strength

4. The appearance of older people might be <u>rejuvenated</u> by transplanting youthful, beautiful skin.

   a. made bolder
   b. made larger
   c. made smaller
   d. made younger

5. Another method that might help the shortage is the keeping of <u>cadavers</u>.

   a. dead bodies
   b. diseased bodies
   c. old bodies
   d. sick bodies

## Writing It Down

Read the following two summaries of the mini-lecture. Choose the *one* summary that best represents the lecture. Then, decide which words are the most important, and arrange them in the note-taking form you want. Discuss your answers.

*Summary #1*

There are not enough organs available for transplants. In the future, this problem might be relieved by substituting one body part for another and by keeping brain-dead bodies alive until their body parts can be used.

*Summary #2*

The use of transplants promises to do much to improve people's lives in the future. Not only will diseased or worn out parts be replaced by transplants, but people's mental abilities, strength, or beauty all might be improved with their use.

I chose Summary #\_\_\_\_\_ .

My notes: _____

_____

_____

_____

_____

 Listen to the mini-lecture one more time. Look at the notes while listening.

## Following Up

1. Go to the library and read the article about transplants in *The Futurist* magazine (May–June 1987).
2. Read the discussion suggestions, and choose one to talk or write about.
   a. Do you know of anyone who has had an organ transplant? Which organ? When was the operation? How is the person's health now?
   b. How would you feel about donating parts of your body to medical science after your death? Do you know anyone who has done that?
3. Read the transcript of the mini-lecture. Highlight the main idea. Highlight any vocabulary that you do not understand, and find the meanings. Listen to the mini-lecture and follow along with the transcript.

TODAY'S LECTURE

Hypothermia

# Before You Listen

## Getting Set

Can you guess what *hypothermia* means without looking at the dictionary?

If *hypo* means "below" and *thermia* means "heat," what do you think the whole word means?

## Talking It Over

You will hear a mini-lecture about hypothermia. Look at the following list of words. Practice saying them. Which words do you think that you will hear? Why? Discuss your answers.

| | |
|---|---|
| birth | heart |
| breathing | hydrogen |
| cold | indoor |
| dancing | outdoor |
| death | oxygen |
| exposure | temperature |

# As You Listen

 **Checking It Off**

Look at the vocabulary list. Listen to the mini-lecture. Circle the words that you hear. Discuss your choices.

## Zeroing In: Main Idea

This mini-lecture has one main idea. Read the following sentences. Put an X in front of the most important point. Discuss your choice.

_____ 1. The biggest danger to people engaged in activities outdoors is hypothermia.

_____ 2. Hypothermia is the condition of the body when the temperature goes below 98.6 degrees Fahrenheit.

_____ 3. Hypothermia is a problem in the springtime or fall.

_____ 4. People die slowly because of wind or rain, or very quickly in cold water.

## Zeroing In: Supporting Details

Read the following details from the mini-lecture. Put an X in front of the _two_ details which support the main idea.

_____ 1. Air temperatures in the spring are 60–70 degrees, while the water temperature is around 50 degrees.

_____ 2. Hunting, fishing, and trapping are outdoor activities.

_____ 3. Hypothermia causes the heart to slow down.

_____ 4. People with hypothermia are not easy to awaken.

_____ 5. The body does not get enough oxygen, making a person feel weak.

# After You Listen

## In Other Words

The following sentences are from the mini-lecture. Look at the underlined words. Practice saying them. Then, choose their meanings.

1. A person becomes listless.
   a. too embarrassed to do anything
   b. too excited to do anything
   c. too poor to do anything
   d. too weak to do anything

2. Their speech becomes slurred.
   a. clear
   b. fast
   c. slow
   d. unclear

3. You start to <u>shiver</u>.

    a. shake
    b. sleep
    c. speak
    d. sweat

4. You <u>doze off</u> and are difficult to awaken.

    a. begin to dream
    b. close your eyes
    c. fall asleep
    d. go to bed

5. The air temperatures are <u>temperate</u>.

    a. both hot and cold
    b. cold
    c. hot
    d. not hot or cold

## Writing It Down

Read the following two summaries of the mini-lecture. Choose the *one* summary that best represents the lecture. Then, decide which words are the most important, and arrange them in the note-taking form you want. Discuss your answers.

*Summary #1*

Hypothermia causes death on land by making the heart stop beating. In water, death comes from drowning because of loss of arm and leg control.

*Summary #2*

Hypothermia describes the body condition when the temperature falls below 98.6 degrees Fahrenheit. As a result, the heart slows down, meaning that the body gets less oxygen which causes weakness.

I chose Summary #_____ .

My notes: _____

_____

_____

_____

_____

Listen to the mini-lecture one more time. Look at the notes while listening.

## Following Up

1. Consult an encyclopedia in the library to find out more about hypothermia. What are some recommended procedures to follow when a person suffers from this condition? Report your findings to the class.

2. Read the discussion suggestions, and choose one to talk or write about.
   a. Hypothermia is one of the main causes of death among the elderly. Why?
   b. Have you ever experienced any of the signs of hypothermia? Where were you? What did you do?

3. Read the transcript of the mini-lecture. Highlight the main idea. Highlight any vocabulary that you do not understand, and find the meanings. Listen to the mini-lecture and follow along with the transcript.

TODAY'S LECTURE

Locusts

# Before You Listen

## Getting Set

Does your country have locusts?

What advantages/disadvantages can you think of for having them?

## Talking It Over

You will hear a mini-lecture about locusts. Look at the following list of words. Practice saying them. Which words do you think that you will hear? Why? Discuss your answers.

| | |
|---|---|
| antennae | insect |
| climate | mammals |
| destroy | migrate |
| food chain | snakes |
| grasshoppers | swarms |
| hop | vegetation |

# As You Listen

 **Checking It Off**

Look at the vocabulary list. Listen to the mini-lecture. Circle the words that you hear. Discuss your choices.

## Zeroing In: Main Idea

This mini-lecture has one main idea. Read the following sentences. Put an X in front of the most important point. Discuss your choice.

_____ 1. Locusts are large grasshoppers.

_____ 2. Locusts eat more than any other insect.

_____ 3. People in Kuwait eat locusts.

_____ 4. Locusts eat the food that people need.

## Zeroing In: Supporting Details

Read the following details from the mini-lecture. Put an X in front of the *two* details which support the main idea.

_____ 1. Locusts are not harmful most of the time.

_____ 2. Locusts can eat hundreds of tons of food per day in a one-square-mile area.

_____ 3. Locusts can destroy all the vegetation in areas they visit.

_____ 4. The dictionary says that locusts are large grasshoppers.

_____ 5. The female locust can lay about 400 eggs during its lifetime.

# After You Listen

## In Other Words

The following sentences are from the mini-lecture. Look at the underlined words. Practice saying them. Then, choose their meanings.

1. Give (locusts) enough <u>moisture</u> for their eggs and their young to develop, and they become a real menace.
   a. food
   b. heat
   c. sun
   d. wetness

2. Give (locusts) enough moisture for their eggs and their young to develop, and they become a real <u>menace</u>.
   a. adult
   b. danger
   c. reward
   d. success

3. The places that (locusts) live in are mostly quite <u>arid</u>.

   a. cold
   b. dry
   c. wet
   d. windy

4. Under the right conditions, (locusts) become the <u>most voracious</u> insects in the world.

   a. drinking the most
   b. eating the most
   c. sleeping the most
   d. traveling the most

5. (Locusts) <u>process</u> their food faster.

   a. digest
   b. eat
   c. find
   d. smell

## Writing It Down

Read the following two summaries of the mini-lecture. Choose the *one* summary that best represents the lecture. Then, decide which words are the most important, and arrange them in the note-taking form you want. Discuss your answers.

*Summary #1*

Locusts have a few good points. This is proven by the fact that they provide food for both human beings and animals in some countries of the world.

*Summary #2*

The terrible thing about locusts is that they take food that millions of people need in order to survive. This is proven by the fact that they kill all growing things in places they visit.

I chose Summary #_____ .

My notes: _____

_____

_____

_____

_____

Listen to the mini-lecture one more time. Look at the notes while listening.

## Following Up

1. Go to the library and read the article on locusts found in the *Aramco World Magazine* (May/June 1987, p. 813).

2. Read the discussion suggestions, and choose one to talk or write about.
   a. Have you ever seen a swarm of insects? Where? How did you feel? What did you do?
   b. Some people eat boiled locusts. Have you ever eaten something unusual like locusts? What? When? Why?

3. Read the transcript of the mini-lecture. Highlight the main idea. Highlight any vocabulary that you do not understand, and find the meanings. Listen to the mini-lecture and follow along with the transcript.